Yogi Dr Samprasad Vinod MD, PhD
meditation all over the world for over 36 years, including India, the USA, the UK and continental Europe. He has written many books, innumerable popular articles in leading newspapers and research papers in international journals. He regularly appears on radio and television in India and Europe. He is a member of the Advisory Board of the Kaivalyadhama Yoga Institute, and a patron member of the Yoga Fellowship of Northern Ireland, Yoga Therapy Ireland and Yoga for Health and Education Trust, UK. He received the coveted National FIE Foundation Award for outstanding contributions to the field of yoga and the Vijayshri Award, which was also given to Mother Teresa. He lives in India.

The foreword is written by the late B.K.S. Iyengar, who was the founder of Iyengar Yoga (which has 180 institutes in over 40 countries) and was one of the most highly respected yoga teachers in the world. He has written many books on yoga practice and philosophy, including international bestseller *Light on Yoga* (which has been translated into 17 languages), *Light on Pranayama* and *Light on the Yoga Sutras of Patanjali*.

In 2004, Iyengar was named one of the 100 most influential people in the world by *Time* magazine. The President of India conferred Padmavibhushan, one of India's highest civilian honours, on Iyengar on 26 January 2014. He left his mortal body on 20 August 2014 for heavenly abode at the age of 95. His worldwide legacy is a monumental body of work in the field of yoga. May his soul rest in peace!

*This book is dedicated
to my revered father
Maharshi Nyayaratna Dhundirajshastri Vinod
and my mother
Maitreyi Vinod*

My father was a true spiritual master. He always cherished the idea of spreading Indian classical wisdom to people across the world. This book is a sincere step in that direction.

Other Books by the Author

Yogi Dr Vinod is the author of 11 successful books on yoga and meditation and one co-authored book on Ayurveda and yoga. *9 Secrets of Successful Meditation* is his first book to be published in English, and is also available in Portuguese.

Mental Health and Peace of Mind, 1998, Anmol Publishers, Pune
Inner Transformation through Shavasan-Meditation, 1998, Anmol
    Publishers, India
The Royal Way to Fulfilment of Aspirations, 1997, Dr Mrs Rujuta Vinod
Meditation – Personal Insights and Guidance, 1999, Anmol Publishers,
    India
Reflections on Yoga, During Travel Abroad, 1999, Pramod Publishers,
    Pune
Being Happy and Sharing it with Others, 1994, Maharshi Vinod
    Research Foundation, Pune
Guidelines for Sharing Happiness with Others, 1994, Maharshi Vinod
    Research Foundation
Yoga and Mind, 2004, Proficient Publishing House, Pune
Yoga Practices (An Inward Journey), 2010, Proficient Publishing House,
    Pune
Mirror of Life, 2011, Proficient Publishing House, Pune
Ayurveda and Yoga Therapy (co-author), 2014, Chaukhamba Sanskrit
    Pratishthan, Delhi

9 SECRETS OF SUCCESSFUL MEDITATION

The Ultimate Key to Mindfulness, Inner Calm and Joy

Dr Samprasad Vinod

Foreword by B.K.S. Iyengar

WATKINS

Sharing Wisdom Since
1893

This edition published in the UK in 2015 by
Watkins, an imprint of Watkins Media Limited
19 Cecil Court, London WC2N 4EZ

enquiries@watkinspublishing.co.uk

Design and typography copyright © Watkins Media Limited 2015
Text copyright © Dr Samprasad Vinod 2002, 2015

Typeset by JCS Publishing Services Ltd, www.jcs-publishing.co.uk

Printed and bound in Europe

British Library Cataloguing in Publication data available

ISBN 978-1-78028-802-4

www.watkinspublishing.com

Contents

Contents

Acknowledgements

I am grateful to the late Yogapitamah (grandfather of yoga) B.K.S. Iyengar Guruji for his Foreword. His appreciation was always a blessing to me. He was associated with our family for more than six decades. He had given demonstrations on yoga during the huge Vyasapooja Mahotsav for three years in a row at the age of 30. My father initiated this unique social programme in 1944 and it was very popular, attended by thousands of devotees from across India and abroad. He started this event to commemorate Vyasa Maharshi, the guru of all gurus.

My grateful thanks also to the late Howard Kent, Director of the Yoga for Health Foundation, UK (now the Yoga for Health and Education Trust), who kindly offered his help when this book was originally published. May his soul rest in peace.

My special thanks to Dr David Frawley alias Vamadeva Shastri for writing a scholarly Introduction in support of this book. I am grateful to scores of my students of yoga from India and abroad who provided the source material.

My warm thanks to Liz Comerton, Lilias Folan and Dr M.L. Gharote for their generous comments and endorsements.

I am indebted to my better half Rujuta, who looked after all the activities of our Yoga Clinic in India, allowing me the free time to write this long-overdue book on meditation.

I acknowledge with thanks the help and encouragement I received from my brothers Dr Hrishikesh, Udayan and my sister-in-law Dr Arundhati. My warm thanks to my friends Dr Subhash Ranade, Ian

Frame, Joy Monkoo and to my yoga students Suneel Chinchanikar, Devendra Kotwal and Shyam Bapat for their help.

I am also grateful to Michael Mann, Kelly Thompson and all the staff at Watkins Publishing for their support.

Foreword

B.K.S. Iyengar

Dr Samprasad Vinod's work on *9 Secrets of Successful Meditation* is well worth reading as he logically presents the rhythmic movements of nature as well as our way of living. This is bound to help one understand the flow of life.

Nature moves rhythmically, but we – as humans bestowed with freedom of thought – create tsunamis and lose the path of rhythm, concord and balance and create disturbances in our thoughts, words and deeds.

We should know that our minds play a dual role in satisfying the needs and greeds of the senses on the one hand, but at the same time like to satisfy their owner – the self. As such, if we open our minds and cultivate friendship with one and all, show compassion to the needy, joy to those who are better off than us, appreciate that we are in a better position compared to those who are underprivileged, and lastly are unconcerned about those who do not improve in spite of guidance, then all these things help us to develop a thought-free state. This thought-free state helps us to reach all pointed attention from one pointed attention.

If one pointed attention is mental concentration (*dharana*), all pointed attention is meditation (*dhyana*). In other words, to remain thoughtfully and uninterruptedly with attentive awareness in a state of thoughtlessness is meditation.

The journey to meditation is easy if the avenue of the mind is clear. If the road is bumpy, one has to laboriously walk or drive carefully. When the road is smooth, however, walking or driving is easy and effortless. In the same way, if the mind is bumpy with distractions and vacillation, the journey towards meditation is hard. If the mind is kept in a thought-free state, then meditation is automatic. When the mind is thought-free, it loses its identity and transforms into a single mind or cosmic mind. While the mind remains single, vibration comes to a standstill. This is meditation.

Dr Samprasad Vinod is helping fellow travellers on the journey to meditation, making the road easy by presenting stories of those who have reached the destination. His work adds flavour to ignite and inspire those who love to be alive in the world of the self, respecting the material world and showing the means to bring the objective wisdom of the world together with the subjective wisdom of the self.

As meditation is a path of evolution in inward attention, this book may help his readers to gain confidence in treading the path of meditation to realize the eternal self that resides within each of us.

B.K.S. Iyengar
Ramamani Iyengar Manorial Toga Institute
31 May 2013

Foreword

If a varied group of people were asked what they thought meditation was and what it involved, the range of answers would almost certainly be weird and wonderful. Until very recently in the West there was a great deal of apprehension about it, and even the rapidly growing number of people joining yoga classes would emphasize that they 'only wanted the exercises'.

Year after year, the stress factor grows. We have entered the twenty-first century urged to accept a creed of greed. This very outlook on life is deeply stressful. If the aim of life is to accumulate more and more – money and possessions – this urge, being driven by the senses, puts body and mind under more and more pressure. The result is that, despite the advances of technology, breakdowns in health become ever more prevalent.

This produces a feeling of unease, which has become an obvious characteristic of our age, and this sense sparks off a search for a way of life which can be calm and peaceful. The practice of meditation – even though it is little understood – is growing rapidly.

It is, of course, important to understand what meditation is *not,* while discovering what it *is* and what fundamental difference it can and will make to our life. In our frenetic society we tend to exclaim: 'Don't just sit there – do something!' Slowly we are learning that a better approach is to say: 'Don't just do something – sit there!'

Yogi Samprasad Vinod comes from a distinguished spiritual family, yet he has the knack of clarifying complicated processes and making them understandable. This book offers a synthesis of his teaching which throws light onto many a dark area. The result is a work which clarifies the subject of meditation. Studied quietly and carefully, the *9 Secrets of Successful Meditation* can bring great benefit to the reader.

Howard Kent
Director, Yoga for Health Foundation, UK

From the Mindshore

A Preface by the Author

This book is essentially a practical guide for all those who are directly or indirectly connected with meditation. It is also meant for those who intend to learn meditation but are novices in the field. It will be very useful for the beginner, as it clearly explains the basic concepts and principles of meditation.

Those who have been practising meditation for several years will find many useful practical suggestions in the book. They can make use of these pearls of wisdom to become more successful in whatever form of meditation they practise. Those who are in the process of developing an interest in meditation will find it inspiring and it will help them to get started on the path.

It is very interesting to see the similarities between different forms of meditation after we have studied one particular form in depth. It is a revelation that opens doors to understanding and insight into the whole subject of meditation. This book is the outcome of my personal efforts in that direction.

The focus of this book is to channel the growing public interest in meditation. My deep interest and involvement in yoga and meditation goes back more than 35 years, although meditation has always been closer to my heart than the physical side of yoga.

My first experience of the highest state of consciousness, or what is conventionally called *nirvikalpa samadhi*, was at the age of 20, when I was a second-year medical student. This single experience completely transformed my life. At that time, I was not familiar with experiences of this kind. Naturally, I could not decide whether it was a true experience of the highest state of consciousness or merely a flight of my imagination. I needed some endorsement and rational explanation.

I searched for someone who could clear my doubts and explain the real meaning and true significance of my experience. I could not find such a person. In fact, I was looking for someone like my father, who was a highly evolved yogi and a true spiritual master. I could have trusted his opinion. He would have either readily endorsed my spiritual experience after confirming its genuineness or would have flatly refused to do so, had he found it imaginary or phoney. Unfortunately, he wasn't around then. He had left his mortal body before I had the experience.

I could not find any other yogi who I thought as capable as my revered father. I thought it was a highly specialized job that required a true expert to guide me. I wanted to consult somebody who had himself reached the highest pinnacle of human experience and was easily accessible to me too. Such people are always difficult to find.

I had two options: either settle for somebody regardless of their spiritual authority, or pursue this on my own. After careful consideration, I chose the second course. I was aware of the hardships that were in store for me. I knew that it was not going to be smooth sailing. However, it turned out to be a very interesting, challenging and fruitful pursuit, which helped me grow and mature through meditation.

Now, when I look back, I sincerely feel that it was the right decision. In fact, it turned out to be a great blessing. I started working on myself to find out the authenticity of my original spiritual experience. I spent a lot of time in determining whether it was a genuine and replicable experience or just an accident. My real quest was to explore whether I could experience it again at will or not.

I was very honest, careful and discerning in my pursuit. I didn't want to mistake an unreal mental state for a real spiritual experience and get misled and lost in the process. I confirmed and reconfirmed by trying one technique of meditation after another until I discovered that they all took me to the same destination, the same state of consciousness. I rationally examined and compared my first experience with the later experiences using other techniques. In the process, I realized that the underlying common principles are the same.

It was hard work, which continued for a long time. But it paid me rich dividends in the form of better understanding of the subtle concepts and processes underlying different forms of meditation. I looked at it as a God-sent opportunity to test and confirm the authenticity and validity of my first experience of *nirvikalpa samadhi*, and to do it again and again using different techniques of meditation. I did my best to make the most of this opportunity.

Occasionally, I would think that my father should have been around to guide me. He could have saved me the lengthy process of 'self-verification'. Had he been around, his mere presence could have influenced the self-motivated exploratory work I was doing that was keeping me intellectually active and spiritually alive. It helped me understand the more profound and deeper dimensions of yoga and meditation.

After years of contemplation, self-study and experimentation, I came to realize that the first experience of *samadhi*, as well as all those that followed, were quite genuine.

Later, I developed an intense urge to share what I knew about yoga and meditation with other people. During a span of some 35 years, I have taught yoga and meditation to thousands of Indian and overseas students. I enjoy teaching meditation immensely. In fact, I never really teach in the conventional sense of the term, but just share my thoughts and experiences with my students and audiences. I dislike taking a position of superiority and authority over my students like a formal teacher or a guru. I don't like to put myself on a pedestal as this would create a serious barrier in communication with them.

I look at my pupils as my close friends. I respect them for who they are and like to see them become what they are capable of. I offer them all possible help, so that they understand and practise meditation more effectively. I like to establish a good rapport and connection with them. Similarly, they feel at home and at ease with me. Soon they open up and start sharing their personal problems and the difficulties they encounter during meditation.

— * —

This book is the outcome of all the interactions between me and my students. It is filled with simple practical guidelines that are easy to understand and bring into practice.

It contains nine fundamental secrets, each one highlighting an important facet of meditation. These aspects are not usually given the emphasis they deserve. In fact, they are the heart and soul of the art and science of meditation. They are the real 'Secrets of Meditation', and can be used to improve the quality of any form of meditation.

The opening chapter emphasizes the importance of taking a broader view of the subject. In the subsequent chapters I have elaborated on various important topics related to meditation to encourage better understanding and practice. The three techniques of meditation that I have studied and experimented with in great depth are included in the Appendix, for reference and use.

As I am male, using he/his comes naturally to me in writing the text. This does not in any way imply disrespect or unconcern for other sexes.

I sincerely hope that you enjoy reading this book and develop a true taste for meditation.

Yogi Dr Samprasad Vinod MD, PhD, DSc (AM)
Email: vinodsamprasad@gmail.com
www.maharshivinod.org
www.patanjalyoga.org

Introduction

Meditation has become a popular topic in thought and healing all over the world today. This has occurred mainly because of the emphasis placed on meditation by great teachers from India in their world travels over the past century. From Swami Vivekananda at the start of the twentieth century to Sri Aurobindo, Ramana Maharshi, Paramahansa Yogananda, the many disciples of Swami Shivananda of Rishikesh, and Maharishi Mahesh Yogi and his Transcendental Meditation movement, the teachers of India have brought the message of meditation to all corners of the globe. Life without meditation is no real life. Without meditation we remain on the surface of our being and cannot contact the real depths of truth and beauty hidden within all of us. Similarly, a culture without a tradition of meditation is a superficial and outward culture that has not yet contacted the wellsprings of life and creativity within.

While the modern world prides itself on education, it is still deficient in training us how to use our minds properly. It lacks a science of consciousness to complement its material sciences. The result is that many people today unnecessarily suffer psychologically, even those who are affluent or well educated. They are victims of their own mental and emotional impulses, which they don't know how to manage, and are ruled by their thoughts. They are prey to suggestions, influence and advertising and don't know who they really are or what their real purpose in life is.

The only solution to such inner unrest and confusion is meditation. Meditation is the key to all lasting happiness because all lasting happiness must reside within us. If it comes from something external we must eventually lose it, however hard we may try to hold on to it. It is never really ours. When we lose a person or object of our happiness, we are left with sorrow and pain. The joy of meditation, on the other hand, can never be lost. It even follows us after the death of the body.

However, the joy of meditation does not come easily. Joy is the long-term reward but seldom the initial experience of meditation. We must first break through the dullness and distraction of the mind in order to reach its deeper bliss. We must calm the surface waves of the mind ocean to reach the deep currents of consciousness behind and beyond the senses. This requires time, patience and depth of both mind and character. If we lack this determination, meditation quickly becomes dry and meaningless.

Meditation is the sovereign way to change our consciousness, to lift us from the dreary sphere of egocentric concerns into the blissful realm of higher awareness. Yet while many people speak of meditation and many practise it, few gain its greater rewards. This is because we often lack the foundation in our life and personality to allow meditation to work for us. Nor does our culture provide the encouragement or support to pursue it. As Yogi Dr Samprasad Vinod so simply and eloquently points out, meditation is our true nature. This idea goes back to the Yoga Sutras of Patanjali.

In his commentary on the first Sutra, Vyasa notes that *samadhi* is the very nature (*dharma*) of the mind (*chitta*). The problem is that the mind has two natures. One part of its nature, its higher aspect or potential, is the capacity for meditation, the mind's love of peace and truth. But the other aspect, its lower nature that we stimulate in our culture, is distraction and impressionability, the mind's capacity to get lost in the external world and its illusions. The mind's higher nature, which manifests when we look within, is meditation, but its lower nature, when we look without, is attachment to external objects, running after the things of the world, which are endless. The mind's true nature, when we keep it free of external influences, is meditation. But the mind's lower nature, when we open it up to external influences, is loss of attention and the very denial of meditation. The mind is very vulnerable and easily influenced. It has a spiritual root but, like fresh fruit, can spoil easily. We must strive to keep it free of the external influences that imbalance it. This is the importance of the *chitta-vritti-nirodha* of Patanjali, controlling the impulses of the mind. Once the mind falls under the influence of sensory indulgences it easily loses its own nature and throws itself away on the world. It is like a child that is improperly educated and grows up with many unnecessary bad habits.

9 Secrets of Successful Meditation is an important work that deals with the problems of meditation and shows practical ways to overcome them. Yogi Dr Vinod points out that it is easy to strain at meditation or to approach it in an artificial way. It is hard to be natural, and attempts to be natural are often among the most contrived things that we can do. The problem is that the ego tries to meditate wilfully and turns meditation into a show or into a battle. One must always be gentle with meditation. The mind is delicate, like a flower, and requires care and consistency in order to calm it.

Meditation techniques are certainly useful but they merely prepare the mind for meditation, as Yogi Vinod notes. Visualizations of beautiful nature scenes or gods and goddesses settle our field of impressions. *Pranayama* gives us additional energy to direct the mind within. Mantras like 'Om' help us counter negative thought patterns and harmonize the mind to higher vibratory frequency. But meditation in essence is simply resting in our true nature and disregarding all other distractions.

Yogi Dr Vinod is an ideal person to write about meditation. He comes from an illustrious family, with his father a yogi of great renown. He has studied and practised yoga and meditation for many years, and has taught meditation to people from all over the world, including Europe and the United States. He is a medical doctor and has also worked with Ayurveda, giving him a profound knowledge of the healing power of meditation on both body and mind. While his teaching is true to the tradition, he speaks in a contemporary idiom that any thoughtful person can easily understand. This book is an important contribution in the field that will clear up many misconceptions and lead people forward in their practice. It will take the reader out of the maze of popular distortions to a simple understanding of the mind and how to transform it. It is notably practical, clear and to the point. It has many important stories, anecdotes and guidelines to follow that make it easy to read, entertaining and insightful. Its step-by-step process makes it a good manual for meditation practice.

9 Secrets of Successful Meditation is bound to enrich anyone's practice of meditation. For many, it will open wide the doors of meditation, which had originally seemed impossible to move.

Dr David Frawley, alias Vamadeva Shastri,
Director, American Institute of Vedic Studies,
Santa Fe, USA

SECRET NUMBER ONE
Take a Broader View

Many years ago, a good friend of mine came to see me in my consulting room. I felt concerned about him as he was looking quite depressed. During our conversation, he told me that he had suffered a bad loss in his business and was feeling totally frustrated. After a long discussion, I took him to the terrace and asked him to lie down on the floor and look at the beautiful blue sky overhead. 'Just let go and relax,' I told him. After a few minutes of relaxation, I said, 'Look at your life from a very high position in the sky. Slowly, come back to your present problem, looking at it from the higher position. After having seen your problem from a wider perspective, don't you realize that you are a little too worried about your problem? Your problem appears bigger, because you are looking at it from the level where it actually exists. If you rise above the problem and look at it afresh from a higher and broader perspective, it will not appear as grave to you as it appears now. A broader perspective will help you understand it better too.'

After another try, he realized the usefulness of this technique and continued to practise it at home. A few weeks later he called me to report that he was feeling much better and was slowly coming out of his depression. He was able to keep his cool and see his problems as part of the bigger picture. Alongside the other measures he employed to deal with his business problems, he regularly used this approach to maintain his inner poise. Gradually, his problems got sorted out, he revived his credit with the bank and eventually did very well in his business.

Frankly speaking, I knew that it was going to work for him. It was only a question of sincerity, application and a genuine desire to make proper use of the method. Therefore, it was not much of a surprise to me. I had successfully used this method before on many of my patients who were suffering from different psychological and psychosomatic problems. It works because it helps the person realize the actual gravity of a given problem in the context of the larger realities of life. Secondly, it helps them understand and have a better perspective on what to do about their health problems.

It is advisable for regular practitioners of meditation, beginners or those who are interested in just knowing more about meditation to take a wider perspective on meditation right from the beginning. To take a broader perspective, we have to pay attention to the basics.

We have to be clear about the fundamental concepts of meditation and related philosophical thoughts before we begin the actual practice and before we take the first step on this path. It would also be worthwhile for those who are already practising some form of meditation to spend some time getting 'refreshed' about these issues.

If we do this exercise in the beginning it goes a long way. It helps us improve the quality of our meditation practice. With a broader perspective, we know how to make use of the knowledge and understanding of meditation in the wider context of life in general and our individual lives in particular. If for some reason we haven't done this exercise before, we must do it now. It is never too late to do something of real value and importance to us. A lack of understanding of meditation can substantially delay our progress on the path. It may also be very difficult to integrate meditation into our daily living. And we should make meditation an integral part of our everyday life – sporadic short-term practice is of very little value. Such practice may never bring the far-reaching spiritual benefits to us. Making meditation part and parcel of our life is in fact a key principle behind learning it. It hardly matters which particular form of meditation we are practising.

Broad-based meditation brings broadness of vision. With broad vision, we can differentiate good meditation techniques from bad ones. This in effect protects us from getting carried away with a particular cult, self-proclaimed guru or religious denomination. Narrowness of vision gives rise to such problems and does more harm than good. That is why we have to take precautions to stay away from such dangers, right from the beginning of our journey. Knowledge of the wider context of meditation helps us do this – if we then happen to come across such problems, we are able to handle them well.

1

Understand the Laws of Nature

Taking a broader view of meditation starts by making friends with nature. Nature can be our best friend, philosopher and guide in this respect if we know how to relate to it. What we need to do is just keep our eyes open and start looking around us. Slowly we develop a rapport, become more meditative and realize the important role played by nature in our life.

It is astounding to see how nature works within the immaculate framework of its eternally incorruptible, infallible and irrefutable laws. They govern our individual existence and everything that surrounds us. By learning from these laws and respecting them, we begin to realize how much they have to offer to us. The secrets of nature are revealed to us, provided we co-operate with its laws.

Once we know how to learn from nature, we can see what 'perpetual learning' really means. Perpetual learning helps us develop better understanding and insight into the basic realities of physical life. While learning from nature, we learn a lot about ourselves, because we are an integral part of the vast cosmic existence. Meditation helps us appreciate this truth.

By being in close proximity to nature, we slowly learn how to become more open. This openness, coupled with our efforts in the appropriate direction, brings a great deal of qualitative improvement in our daily practice of meditation.

Interdependence

It seems that the operation of the universe is governed by intelligent design. It works in accordance with the 'Law of Interdependence'. Every single part of existence is so designed that it will be of some help to another part, and the part that receives such help will reciprocate it whenever its turn comes. For this model to work smoothly, the creatures that help each other also depend on each other for that help. For example, plants give out oxygen – which they do not need for their own survival – and in return they take in carbon dioxide, which they do need. The plants get rid of something non-essential to them, but it is vital for human survival. Similarly, human beings give out carbon dioxide, which they don't need for their survival, but it is essential for plants.

The fascinating underlying reality is that it is easier to part with something that one doesn't want than with something one badly wants. Stale vegetables, spoiled food, faecal excreta, etc. are harmful waste products that are of no use to humans. What is harmful, poisonous and life-threatening to humans is highly nutritious, life-giving, precious food for the plants.

The secret behind this wonderful design is that plants and human beings help each other survive and grow in such a manner that helping each other is not a big burden on them. Similarly, a meditator should realize that receiving help from others and giving help to others is a built-in characteristic of nature. Therefore, he/she need not feel shy of receiving help from others nor should they feel proud when they offer help to others.

After regular practice of meditation, one begins to know oneself better. Usually, after knowing himself, a meditator wants to share his knowledge of meditation with others. While sharing, he should never let his ego get too inflated. As a matter of fact, there is no reason to feel egoistic about the sharing, because one who shares also benefits from such sharing.

Through this sharing, space is created within oneself, which gets filled with fresh knowledge. Moreover, one can share only what is already known through personal experience. What one already knows about meditation is in a way no longer useful to oneself. Naturally, what one shares with others is something that one doesn't need for oneself anymore so what we are doing is in line with the Law of Nature. If you part with something that is not useful to you, there is no reason why you should feel proud about it. Pride of any kind can damage the quality of our meditation practice.

So, being of help to each other is a Law of Nature. It is wiser not to fight against this law, but to willingly co-operate with it. It is therefore in our best interest to develop a genuinely helpful attitude towards other people and other creatures.

Independence and Interdependence

It is fascinating to see the harmonious co-existence of the Law of Independence and the Law of Interdependence. Apparently they are poles apart, but still they complement each other. Every creature has a free will through the Law of Independence to make its own choices but, while doing so, it has to stay within the confines of the Law of Interdependence.

Interestingly, on the one hand two opposites like independence and interdependence work together in harmony with each other, and on the other hand they work against each other. Yet there is a subtle balance between the two. The Law of Interdependence applies to all creatures and living beings alike, from a tiny worm crawling under our feet, to the carefully grown shrubs in a garden, to the trees in a forest. It is applicable to everything, wild and domesticated.

By looking at the great symbiosis of independence and interdependence, we can learn an important lesson. It is true that we can protect and preserve our individual independence of choice, but while doing so we have to appreciate that other people are also doing the same thing and we need to respect their independence too.

Man's Menacing Greed

Although interdependence is an inevitable law of nature, it seems that we human beings are willing neither to accept nor respect it. We have become so greedy, so selfish, that we treat Mother Nature as our own personal property. We go on finding new ways and means to exploit her all the time.

We covet everything that is produced in nature. Our greed is boundless. We are not satisfied with all the land that is available to us. We keep excavating everything that is underground. We want to extract all the petroleum from underground reservoirs. We also want to excavate all the minerals, inorganic material, and metals. From the oceans we take out fish, lobsters, pearls – whatever we can lay our hands on. We are unconcerned about the fast denudation of the rich forests. We want to strip everything from the trees: we want their flowers, fruits, leaves and trunks, as well as their roots. We want to suck the animals dry without leaving any milk for their offspring, for whom it is really produced. We want to eat their eggs and flesh. We strip off their skin, extract their teeth, and use their bones and fur.

Our greed is growing day by day in exponential proportions. It seems that we have completely lost our sense of balance and our thoughts and actions have lost their way. We are only concerned about the welfare of humans, to the detriment of the welfare and survival of the rest of the world and its creatures. We are doing this with complete disregard to the fundamental Law of Interdependence. We are taking everything from nature, but not giving anything back. We conveniently forget that, just as we need different things from nature, nature needs certain things from us in return. We are supposed to take proper care of nature and ensure its welfare too.

Being greedy is truly dangerous for us. It is like digging our own graves ready for a premature death. Greed tends to perpetuate through overindulgence. Overindulgence depletes precious life energy from us and leaves us impoverished in the end. As a result, we become slaves to our senses. Through such self-induced slavery, we exploit ourselves and suffer.

The best way to care for nature is to keep our needs and desires within reasonable limits. First of all, we have to decide what is truly reasonable and what is not so reasonable. It must, however, be an honest search to discern the faint line of demarcation between need and greed. It is quite possible that what appears reasonable to us may appear quite unreasonable to others and vice versa. But such things are bound to happen. As long as we are true and honest to ourselves, it hardly matters whether other people approve of our choice or not.

A meditator should always be aware of the compassionate providence of nature. If we could nurture a sincere feeling of gratitude towards nature, it would go a very long way to help us in being successful in meditation.

Create a Chain of Co-operation

The genius of the Creator has masterminded the smooth running of His creation. One of the operating principles is an intelligent interlocking of the individual and collective interests and wellbeing of all creatures and objects.

If one person starts losing balance, everybody else starts losing balance too. Nobody likes to fall. Naturally, everybody comes forward to offer support to the one who is falling, so as to avoid the mishap. In fact, what one does in such situations is to help oneself under the guise of helping others.

The Creator knows that if there is a very strong survival instinct in the minds of human beings, they will protect themselves whenever there is a threat to their lives. Moreover, if the one whose life is in danger knows that by helping others he is going to protect himself from the possible threat to his life, he is bound to go out of his way to protect others. That is how the whole of creation with all its creatures survives. The Creator is very much aware that people will help each other only when their life is in danger – however, for the subsistence of creation, He keeps them bound by the Law of Interdependence. If they have to help each other for their own survival, they will have no choice but to give such help.

Many politicians from India probably learn their shrewdness from the Creator. They form a chain of political friends from different parts of the country. Those who are part of this chain add new shackles to keep it alive and growing. If for some reason a shackle or two gets loose and starts falling apart, the friends come forward to rescue the person from falling. It looks like a great sense of fraternity and commitment.

But through such 'help', they 'help' themselves guard their individual vested interests, under the guise of brotherhood and friendship.

A meditator must understand and willingly accept the Law of Interdependence, so that his individual welfare and wellbeing will always be automatically protected. He has to create a chain of cooperation with fellow practitioners of meditation through such acceptance.

Unfortunately, we human beings do not willingly accept the fact that all things that have been created, whether living or non-living, animate or inanimate, need each other. It is in our own interest to respect the Law of Interdependence and learn to live with it. But under the stupefying influence of ignorance, the human race is currently involved in an indiscriminate plundering of all natural resources. In the process, the genuine needs of those essential parts of the Creation are completely overlooked or ignored.

Freedom of Choice

The quality of life we live and the number of problems we face can depend on how we make use of our freedom of choice.

It is entirely up to us how we make use of the privilege of living – whether we neglect our body and ruin our health or take proper care of it. We have to make an intelligent use of the freedom of choice that is given to us by nature.

As a parallel, giving light and giving shock are two qualities of an electric current. If we do not treat it with care, we will have to face the consequences of our decision. If we are careless in how we use it, it can hurt us. If we decide to protect ourselves from the electric current and make use of the same energy constructively to light a table lamp or put on a fan, electricity will offer us a service.

The Laws of Nature are Incorruptible

The Laws of Nature are absolutely flawless. We can never change them. If we offer a monetary bribe to a deity whom we worship every day and who represents these laws or if we religiously visit a temple, mosque or church doesn't mean that the laws will change.

Similarly, if a rich man offers all his wealth to the Lord, it does not mean that he will be saved from the incurable disease he is suffering. In the same way, if a poor person is not in a position to offer anything to the Lord, it doesn't mean that he is going to die a premature death. The supreme intelligence of the all-pervasive life principle – or nature or God or what you will – is far beyond all such corruption. It is beyond our limited power of comprehension.

Any attempt at bribery is a sure sign of ignorance. It is impossible that the Higher Power will ever succumb to any bribery whatsoever, because it would be like breaking His own laws. He knows that it would create chaos in His creation, and He would never do that. Of course there is nothing wrong in seeking temporary psychological support and solace through prayers, particularly when we are in distress and turmoil. But it is unwise to depend entirely on such help. Prayer can never be a substitute for our own well-directed sincere efforts to overcome our problems. Our prayer must go hand in hand with our efforts.

Nature's Role in a Business

I think the greatest 'businessman' is the one who has created this universe. He is eternally busy producing infinite variety and number of the most beautiful products that are parts of His creation. The most astonishing thing about this businessman is the unbelievable level of perfection. He has achieved in spite of the continuous and never-ending production line. He maintains complete harmony, incredible smoothness and flawless accuracy in all the products of His creation. Incidental minor aberrations in those products are more due to individual mistakes than mistakes committed by Him. We can learn a lot from this 'businessman' and profit from this understanding by applying those principles to our own business.

I know one person who has been doing this. He loves nature. He loves trekking, hiking, mountaineering and skiing. He is a successful businessman. He often says that he has learned a lot by regularly going on nature trails. He also says that he has learned more from nature's classroom than the human one. I often wonder how he finds the time to pursue such exhausting hobbies. He explains that he gets instantly refreshed by being in close proximity to nature. Being in tune with nature has been more rewarding to him than anything else in his life. He has absorbed patience, planning and law abidance from Mother Nature. Looking at the successful business he is running, it is quite obvious that he knows what he is talking about.

Like this businessman, to be successful in our meditation practice we have to closely observe nature and learn from it. We have to start by looking at ourselves to find out what is our nature, before we start observing the nature that surrounds us. Once we are clear about our natural propensities and inclinations, we can start exploring the available techniques of meditation to select one or more that appear suitable to our nature. Then, we can start practising them one by one, to see which one has the best practical application and utility in our day-to-day living. Thereafter, we can focus our attention on the best one, improving its quality and keep refining and perfecting it.

After achieving an adequate degree of proficiency in meditation, we have to continue doing it further, to develop a total understanding about its relevance in modern living. Once we reach such understanding, we can start sharing with others what we really know and personally experience. Constant vigilance about quality will still be necessary. Staying in touch with others who have learned meditation from us is a great joy. It keeps our motivation and interest alive; it inspires others to practise meditation further.

We have to evolve an accurate method to assess the level of perfection we have reached in meditation and try to adhere to it, while doing self-appraisal and appraisal of others. Personal whims and idiosyncrasies have no place in meditation. Such matters can influence our unbiased self-assessment and judgement. We have to be practical and realistic in this regard.

A serene atmosphere in the proximity of nature and keeping the company of like-minded people is essential for spiritual growth through meditation. False praise and appeasement of the ego are detrimental to this purpose. We have to observe quality while learning meditation for ourselves and subsequently when we pass it on to others. Thus, we do not bring a bad reputation to the art and science of meditation. Being quality conscious in meditation means being focused on doing it properly and not being worried about the results. The results will follow, if we are doing it right. Quality also means being clear in theory and practice. Quality depends on 'how' we do it, not 'what' we do. If we understand the philosophy and are in the right frame of mind while doing it, quality comes naturally.

India has come a long way over millennia in the field of yoga and meditation. Over the past several thousand years, the spiritual masters from India have perfected many techniques of meditation. They have been very generous in making those techniques available to the world at large. These time-tested techniques are being used by millions of people from all over the world. Interestingly, meditation is more of an internal state, which is not readily visible at the physical level, apart from certain minor physical actions we perform during its practice.

Apart from the techniques of meditation, India has produced great spiritual masters such as Bhagwan Vyasa, Patanjali, Bhagwan Buddha, Mahavir, Ramana Maharshi, J. Krishnamurti, Vivekananda, Yogi Aurobindo, to name a few. In this sense, India is the spiritual leader of the world. It will therefore be wise on our part to confirm that the meditation technique we intend to learn and follow has an authentic Indian connection to it. When I say Indian connection, I do not mean that whatever is labelled 'Indian' is necessarily authentic and good. We have to verify and confirm it. The important thing is to understand the basics with true clarity and not be gullible or mechanical about it.

2

Meditation Should Help us Solve our Problems

The yogis and spiritual masters say from their personal experience that the sole mission of human life is to discover the true self or *atman* within us. '*Atman*' is the name for the divine energy or life principle within us. They maintain that the real and lasting answer to all human problems, both material and spiritual, lies in the knowledge of the true self. To achieve that, we have to remove the veil of ignorance and make our vision crystal clear so that we can see the true self within us. After such realization the reins of our life get shifted from our limited ego or false self to the unlimited or true self. Consequently, all problems that are caused by our limited self get resolved forever. It is not that the problems cease to exist, but we are able to handle them with poise and efficiency. Nothing else works on a permanent basis like the knowledge of the true self does. The realized souls, yogis and liberated masters from all over the world have been saying this for many ages. They also assert the important role played by meditation in this venture.

One wonders whether what they say is really true. Is meditation really a panacea for all our problems?

Meditation Provides a Broader Outlook

If a realized master says that self-knowledge is a panacea for all human problems it must be true, because he is among the rarest of the rare ones who speaks what he knows through his personal experience. If he says something it is not merely a statement of his belief, but his personal experience that he shares with us. Furthermore, he 'knows' for sure that anybody can live a problem-free life like his if one undertakes a consistent and serious practice of yoga.

A problem-free life doesn't mean a complete 'absence' of all problems. Problems do come and go as long as we are alive, regardless of whether we practice meditation or not. But there is a difference in the manner in which most people face, understand and relate to a given problem and the way a serious student of meditation does. Basically, the difference is in their attitude and approach towards life.

Most people get anxious about their trivial problems, because they do not understand how to 'know' their problems well. But a true yogi knows how to 'know' a problem and therefore remains unperturbed, even under the most trying conditions of life, facing complicated problems with ease and efficiency. He stays unruffled under all circumstances, because he knows how to take a holistic perspective on life. He therefore handles his problems with great ease, confidence, authority and conviction. Meditation *is* certainly a panacea for such yogis – it is their first-hand experience and application of meditation in daily living that works wonders. They live what they preach and preach what they live.

If we carefully study the biographies of realized masters, we learn that many began life in much the same way as everyone else, but managed to rise to the highest peak of human experience through determination, dedication, hard work and perseverance. Regular practice of meditation made all the difference and gradually they evolved into better human beings. Consequently, they could look at themselves, their problems and the world around them in a much more profound and healthy manner. Developing such a comprehensive and all-inclusive outlook towards life is in fact the very reason why we should learn meditation.

After having resolved their personal problems for good, the realized souls such as Buddha or Christ or Mohammed or Mahavir or other prophets develop natural empathy for the whole world. It is not a fake empathy that can be enacted through effort, but a true empathy that comes spontaneously as a natural consequence of self-knowledge.

It grows further into a genuine urge to share what they know and understand about peaceful and happy living with others who are still suffering. This care and concern for others is not restricted to those they are close to, but incorporates the whole of existence.

How Problems Come Into Being

It is very interesting to see how problems emerge in the first place. When do we say that a particular problem is solved? What do we mean exactly by a problem?

The number of problems we face largely depends on how we relate to our environment and ourselves. We face fewer problems if we take a realistic view of life, and more if it is unrealistic. In fact, an unrealistic approach towards life is the root cause of all our individual problems and the problems we create for others.

For example, most of us have average looks. We might improve them slightly by making use of cosmetics, but not much more than that. So why worry about something that is such a widespread problem? Why not accept it and live with it? Why not pay more attention to improving our inner beauty and wellbeing? It is much wiser to do that, isn't it?

Similarly, if an 'average' student aspires to achieve a Stanford or Cambridge doctorate, he is probably asking too much from himself. More than likely, his ambition will not be fulfilled. Severe frustration, followed by an inevitable failure, is probably in store for him. But if he takes a realistic view of his abilities and plans his career accordingly, the chances of success would certainly be brighter. Why not do something one enjoys and is capable of doing? It is much better to pursue an interesting option in life and derive happiness and satisfaction from it.

We all have an inbuilt tendency to give personal reactions to pleasant and unpleasant experiences in our life. This is often responsible for our problems. We all know that life can never be smooth sailing. Sometimes it brings pleasure and sometimes suffering. Most of us like to hold onto pleasures and run away from suffering. It is a natural human tendency to do that, but nevertheless it is one of the key causes of our problems.

We seldom have any dilemma when going through a pleasant experience. Similarly, there is hardly any difficulty in deciding to avoid unpleasant experiences. Problems do not exist if we are mentally prepared to face an unpleasant situation squarely, whenever it comes. But problems come in plenty if we do not get pleasure according to our expectations. Problems also come if we have to confront an unpleasant situation unexpectedly.

Reactions Breed Problems

We do not normally have too many problems while going through pleasant experiences, but they start appearing if we begin to have personal reactions to the absence of such experiences. The moment we begin to hold on to a pleasant experience for an extended period of time, or expect to have the same experience over and over again, the problems start emerging. Thus, our problems depend more on how we respond to pleasures than the actual pleasures themselves. After experiencing pleasures repeatedly, we develop a craving for them. Later, if the same pleasures are denied us, we start facing problems.

The story of a beggar is quite apt in this regard. A pious lady from one town used to regularly give some food to a beggar. Every time he came to her house for the alms, she would give him ample food. After a few days, she started taking him into account when cooking for her family. This practice continued for few weeks. Now the beggar didn't have to run around in search of food. Every day he would go to the same house and get a sufficient quantity of freshly prepared food to satisfy his appetite. Gradually, the beggar got used to it. He felt that everything was now assured to him. He thought that now he was settled in his 'profession'. It started showing on his face. He put on some weight too.

After a few weeks, he completely forgot that he was a beggar and began to feel that it was his 'right' to get food from that house. One day, after receiving his daily quota of alms, he told the housewife, 'I would like to have a large chocolate cake for tomorrow.' She asked him, 'Why? What's the matter? Why do you want a cake?' She was shocked when she heard him say, 'I am tired of the routine food. I want a change.

Tomorrow is my birthday and I am expecting some fellow beggars to come round and celebrate it!'

We may laugh at this beggar. But aren't we all sailing in the same boat? Initially, the beggar was asking for some food for his survival, but later on he began to take it for granted. Are we not doing the same thing when we keep pursuing pleasures? Don't we get used to pleasures and look forward to having them more and more? Don't we constantly cling to them? Get attached to them?

Meditation Helps us Understand our Environment and Ourselves

Broadly speaking, meditation is a panacea for all our problems. With proper practice of yoga and meditation, we first learn how to establish good rapport with ourselves and then with our environment. By doing so we develop a realistic and practical perspective of life. Now we don't have to worry about our problems. We are capable of handling them well whenever they appear.

When can we really say that a particular problem is solved? Firstly, when it is actually solved. Secondly, when we realize that it cannot be solved. And thirdly, when we transcend or go beyond that problem.

Solvable Problems

Unemployment can be a major problem for young people. Meditation can help solve this. Meditation essentially involves self-observation and self-study. With regular practice of meditation, a young person will better understand his likes and dislikes, capabilities and weakness. Moreover, meditation will help him grow in self-awareness, which would be useful in making good choices from the career options that are available to him.

He may have to review earlier career decisions in the light of this self-study and decide what he really wants to do, whether he may want to run a business himself or go for a job.

If he settles on doing a job, he will have to think about the relevant issues like which job, where, whether such jobs are readily available or not, at what remuneration, and so on. After an evaluation of the situation and proper planning, he will have to search for a suitable job at a suitable place where he would like to do it. If he is practising meditation regularly, he will be able to do this exercise better and make the right choice about the job too.

After the initial exercise is over, he will need to send applications to several places to have a wider choice of jobs to choose from. It will then be easier for him to reach the final decision. Then he will have to prepare for interviews and face them confidently. The boundless energy and inner strength that are by-products of meditation will be of great help to him in this connection.

If for some reason he doesn't get the job of his choice, he mustn't lose heart or stop his efforts. He must learn from experience and keep searching for another job until he finds one. A meditative mind will help him take success and failure in his stride without losing confidence. We need an ego-free, pliable mind to learn from our mistakes and failures. In such endeavours patience is always a great virtue. Meditation instils these qualities in us.

After the first exercise of considering what he wants, he may decide not to go for a job but to start a business. He needs to give careful thought to this decision. Once the decision is reached, he must quietly make well-directed and persistent efforts to reach the goal. Single-mindedness of purpose is yet another quality of a meditative mind.

Problems Beyond Solution

There are some extremely difficult problems that defy all solutions in spite of our sincere and persistent efforts to solve them. In such situations, it is much better to willingly accept the problem as it is and learn to live with it. For a meditative mind, which is married to reality, acceptance of the inevitable is very easy.

Cancer is one such problem. It is not only a problem for the patient who suffers from it, but also for his family. It is true that there is a lot of research going on in the world to fight this evil, but as of today, the scientists haven't been able to find a cure for this highly menacing human affliction. It can often be better for a cancer patient to quietly accept the situation and learn to live with it as best one can. I do not say this in a negative sense – I am only offering a very practical solution to the problem. This can reduce associated difficulties like running around in search of alternative remedies and the frustrations that follow an indiscriminate use of such treatments.

I know that this is easier said than done. I also know that giving advice to others is very easy, but when it comes to doing it yourself it can be difficult to put such advice into practice. But, with an unsolvable problem, the best we can do is to reduce its intensity. We have to follow a wise saying: 'While solving a problem, start doing what you can; accept it without any resistance if you can't, and have the wisdom to know the difference between what you can and what you can't do.'

We fear death because the mind likes to live in a state of continuum and death is an irrevocable break in this perpetuity. Our dread of death is because of our lack of familiarity with it. Meditation helps us come face to face with nothingness. It is this nothingness that makes us anxious about death. Regular experience of nothingness through meditation prepares us for death. We may therefore say that problems beyond solution can't be solved, but their intensity can certainly be reduced by accepting them wholeheartedly as they are.

It goes without saying that although we as individuals may need to accept cancer as an unsolvable problem, at a collective level, in the interest and welfare of humanity as a whole, research workers and research scientists should not consider any human problem like cancer to be unsolvable. Otherwise, all the valuable research they are doing in the field would come to an end.

Don't Turn Simple Problems into Complex Ones

I often come across promising young people who tend to take one or two failures to heart and begin to feel frustration and dejection. Despite their persistent efforts, they are not able to break out of their despondency.

Most of them blame unfavourable circumstances or unfair practices adopted by the authorities or some other factors. They seek false solace in false excuses. Some of them make wild generalizations and begin to question their abilities. The most harmful generalization of all is to think that you are good for nothing because you have failed in one or two exams. This may actually convert a solvable problem into an unsolvable one, because they don't know how to assess it or arrive at a proper conclusion.

Meditation helps us create an unshakeable faith in our abilities. It gives us patience to wait until the right opportunity comes along. Most importantly, it strengthens our realistic self-confidence. I can say this with conviction, because I know that it works. I have been counselling young people to help them solve their problems for the past 35 years or so.

There are quite a few meditators who have similar problems. Some of them don't do well in meditation in spite of their sincere efforts. They lose heart after a few failures, because they think that they are not getting anywhere. They also make wild generalizations about their capacity to learn and practise meditation. They usually blame everybody else except themselves for their failures.

One important reason behind writing this book is to offer some convincing solutions to such problems.

SECRET NUMBER TWO
Know What Meditation is Not

After having discussed the importance of taking a broader view of meditation and how it helps us solve our day-to-day problems, now we should understand what meditation *is not*.

Knowing what meditation is not is a prelude to knowing what it *is* and to appreciating it.

It saves us from wasting precious time and energy in pursuing wrong methods of meditation – the same energy can then be used for practising regularly and for achieving deeper levels of meditation.

1

It is Not a Forced Concentration of Mind

Frustration Due to Failure in Meditation

Many years ago, as I was finishing my discourse on meditation, a man in his sixties came forward and asked me a question. 'Dr Vinod, I have been regularly practising meditation for the past several years, but I have never experienced the kind of peace of mind you have been talking about. Do you think I have been doing something drastically wrong? Will you kindly guide me?'

He attracted the attention of the audience, mainly because he was a learned man, almost double my age and yet he was very keen on learning something from me. This was an unusual situation in India in those days – it was rare that a learned man would publicly share his failure and frustration with someone almost half his age.

First of all, it is hard to admit that one might have made a mistake. It is difficult enough to accept our mistake in private, but it is extremely difficult to accept it publicly. It requires a great deal of courage to declare our ignorance and admit our failure. This gentleman's eagerness to correct the mistake and learn something new was highly praiseworthy.

The majority of people prefer to remain imprisoned within their own egos: they remain buried in graves of their creation. They do not even realize that living under the influence of an ego is like living in a world of illusion and imagination. By doing so, they do themselves more harm than good.

Those who happen to realize this truth are not always capable of bringing about any change in their life, nor can they change the lives of others around them. This is because their realization is often too superficial and is therefore quite ineffective in changing anything. Fortunately, this gentleman had no such problems. As the main obstacle of the ego was not present, it was very easy for me to relate and establish communication with him. He appeared to be very receptive to my advice.

It was evident from what he subsequently told me that he had been following a conventional method of meditation. During meditation he was trying in vain to focus his attention on the idol of Lord Ganesh.

Idol worship is a profound and powerful concept. It is in fact a precious gift from the Indian sages to the whole world. This method of worship is common in India. It is relatively easy to settle one's mind on something concrete and comprehensible like an idol rather than the incomprehensible infinite vastness of abstract reality. Idol worship can be extremely useful, provided it is done with a great deal of clarity and understanding about what one is doing while performing the rituals related to such worship. Many people do not know what it is all about. They are not aware of the basics and their idol worship is reduced to mere mechanical repetition of few rites and rituals.

This man was learned but was not an enlightened person. For nearly 20 years, he had been trying 'too hard' to concentrate on the idol of Lord Ganesh but was still not able to get anywhere, despite his sincere efforts. The quality and depth of his meditation never showed any improvement.

It seemed to me that he was an example of the hundreds of thousands of people who have been mistaking mental concentration for meditation and are therefore not getting anywhere.

Effort-Free, Tension-Free Concentration
There is no need to put in so much effort to achieve mental concentration during meditation. In fact, meditation, as is commonly believed, is not a matter of achievement. It is truly a matter of happening. Focusing our

mind on doing things that we really love to do is always easy. When we are deeply interested in doing something with all our heart and mind involved in it, and when we feel highly satisfied doing it, then finding time for it is never a big problem. We don't have to exert too much energy while doing such activities.

Sawai Gandharva Music Festival is a mega event for those who love to listen to Indian classical music. It is held every year in Pune, near Mumbai (formerly Bombay). It is the Indian equivalent of the Boston Pops concerts held in Boston or the Three Tenors concerts in Paris. Many internationally well-known singers and instrumentalists like Pandit Jasraj, Pandit Shivkumar Sharma and Zakir Husain love to attend and give their live performances during this prestigious music show. Those who get an opportunity to come to the dais feel highly honoured to be there. They feel very fortunate to be selected to present their art during this festival.

Thousands of people from all over India and many Indian classical music lovers from abroad attend. I know quite a few music enthusiasts who commute every day from Mumbai to Pune (150 kilometres) to attend the show for the whole night and still manage to go to work in Mumbai the next morning, during the whole ten days of the festival.

The fans love to listen to the music so much that they do not mind all the hardships, the weather and the overcrowding they experience. While listening to music they don't need to make special efforts to remain focused on listening. They are so completely absorbed in the 'divine treat' on those nights that their minds hardly wander. But when it comes to doing a bit of extra work in the office, they find it too boring or feel too tired to do it. They are unable to attend to their work properly and tend to make lots of mistakes. They make excuses to avoid such work, and their efficiency levels drop significantly.

What is true with music fans is also true with sports fans. Sport is a neo-religion for millions of people. They love watching it so much that they remain glued to their TV sets and miss their meals whenever their team is playing. While they are watching the game, nothing else distracts or disturbs them. Noisy traffic, people fighting and shouting and children playing and yelling do not make any difference.

But when it comes to studying, they are unable to focus their attention in the same way. Now, the slightest sound matters a lot. The same boys and girls, who can be totally absorbed in doing something they love to do, suddenly start feeling bored and tired.

The same principle applies to meditation. Until we have a genuine liking for meditation, we have to make a special effort to concentrate. But once we develop a true taste for meditation, no such effort is necessary. Concentration of mind comes automatically and effortlessly on its own. No exertion is needed. There is no need to apply any force to reach the higher states of awareness through meditation.

2

It is Not for a Select Few

Beating One's Own Drum

Many people think that meditation is only meant for a select few people. I was once attending a course on meditation by someone who was well known for his excellent oratory. As I watched him and listened to him, I could sense an air of arrogance in his words, persona, body language and the manner of his speech. The person who introduced him to the audience spoke with great admiration and adoration for the revered speaker. He mentioned that the speaker had been born into a pious family of a great spiritual heritage and learning. He also talked about the early childhood signs of greatness in the speaker, and gave vivid descriptions of his childhood mischief, his dislike for study, lack of interest in formal education, progress on the path of meditation, the first experience of *samadhi* and so on.

The focus of the introduction was not so much on essential information about the speaker to make the audience more receptive to him. It was more than that. He wanted to impress upon the audience that the speaker was not an ordinary person. He belonged to a special category of exceptional people who are 'chosen' to perform a special mission in this world. It was as if the world, filled with ignorant and downtrodden people, had been waiting patiently for his arrival. In short, it was a momentous occasion for the audience to be able to listen to the precious words of this great man.

Early Criticism, Appreciation Later

I am amazed and, to a large extent, amused by such introductions. Once somebody becomes successful in the eyes of the people, everybody starts praising and appreciating such a person for whatever he/she did, regardless of whether it was right or wrong. In fact, this spiritual master must have been a very difficult child, who was severely punished and scolded by his teachers at school. But, now his punishable 'naughtiness' suddenly becomes a 'praiseworthy mischievousness'. His poor performance in formal education becomes a distinct sign of creativity. The same teachers who were once disappointed with his academic performance now start saying that his lack of interest was in fact a sign of exceptional intelligence which is only found in extraordinary people.

As a child, Sachin Tendulkar, the great star of Indian cricket, probably practised some shots that broke the glass windows of the apartment house where he lived. At that time, the neighbours must have got angry with him and complained to his parents about his naughtiness. Some of them might have even made a few demeaning and nasty comments about his future prospects as a cricketer. But now that he has proven his talent as one of the best batsmen in the world who can be compared only with the all-time great Sir Don Bradman, the same neighbours would quickly change their stance and start proudly quoting those instances as early signs of his being a child prodigy and a genius of this century. Everything that he did as a child suddenly becomes a matter of appreciation. In the years to come, when he becomes the greatest batsman that the history of cricket has ever produced, they will start praising him more and more.

What pained me most in the speaker's introduction was that it might have created the wrong impression in the minds of those who listened to him. It sounded as if the field of yoga was so exclusive that it was reserved only for special people.

The history of humanity has seen great people like Isaac Newton, Albert Einstein, Abraham Lincoln, Mahatma Gandhi, Mother Teresa, Leo Tolstoy and Bertrand Russell, who have left lasting marks of the work they have done for the welfare of humanity as a whole. Surprisingly, they were all very simple people, with no air of superiority about them.

Mahatma Gandhi was remarkable because he never posed as a great leader. He never expected any special treatment from others. He was always ready to relate to all kinds of people regardless of their class, creed, religion or nationality. He chose to lead his life like an ordinary person and refused to be deified. This particular attitude of his was a testimony to being a truly extraordinary person.

It is for All

Many thoughts flooded my mind after listening to the exaggerated introduction by the compere. I wondered why meditation should be treated as a monopoly of a handful of chosen people? After all, if meditation is a state of 'no-thought awareness' or a complete silence of mind or being in tune with the core self, why should it be reserved for only a select few? If all human beings possess the same organ, called the mind, then why should freedom from thoughts be a prerogative of just a few?

We are all born with an ability to breathe air into our lungs. This ability stays with us as long as we are alive and we all breathe the same air. We all possess one pair of feet and other organs of the body. How we make use of those organs may vary from person to person, but the basic composition of organs remains the same in all.

Each one of us is bestowed with a wonderful organ called the mind. It is true that some of us possess a sharper mind than others do. Some are able to think more wisely and more deeply than others do. But it is clear that we all possess this precious gift from Mother Nature from the time we were born. How we use it is entirely up to us. Therefore, it is not necessarily the case that those who do not have a sharp mind at present will never be able to develop such sharpness in future. Maybe they will have to wait a little longer or they will be required to put in more sustained effort than those who are blessed with sharp minds.

Everybody has the potential to reach a state of no-thought awareness. Nobody is special in this respect. All of us have an equal opportunity to experience higher states of consciousness through meditation.

I am reminded of an interesting anecdote. A client goes to a lawyer and asks his advice: 'What should I do to get a divorce?'

The lawyer enquires, 'Are you married?'

The client replies, 'Yes.'

'Then you don't have to do anything else. You will get the divorce,' assures the lawyer.

The point of the story is that those who have a mind can surely be divorced from the mind. They can be free of its influence on their being through proper practice of meditation. Everybody can learn and practise meditation – there is nothing special about it.

3

Meditation is Certainly Not Difficult

Pride and Ego Satisfaction

I was once attending a weekly group meeting of *sadhakas*. *Sadhakas* are dedicated practitioners of meditation. They were having a *satsang*, a special kind of gathering for spiritual learning. It is supposed to be an informal and intimate meeting of like-minded people who are deeply interested in the exchange of ideas, thoughts and experiences about meditation and other spiritual practices. *Satsang* is a great opportunity for true learning by sharing experiential understanding with each other.

It should be conducted in a friendly, informal, ego-free, mutually respecting and caring atmosphere. The atmosphere should allow and encourage free expression from all the participants. Most importantly during *satsang* the dictum is – do not fight, but interact; do not debate, but discuss.

Unfortunately, it seldom happens that way. People usually tend to miss the essential and get caught up in the superfluous. This is precisely what was happening in that group. It was not a real *satsang* because it was a mixed group of *sadhakas*. Some of them had been regular practitioners of meditation for many years. Some were beginners and the rest were curious enthusiasts who were novices in the field. One of the senior *sadhakas* among them was their leader. He was in charge of the deliberations. I was present there only as a silent observer and a quiet listener.

The main topic of their discussion was whether meditation was easy or difficult to practise. Most of the senior members were of the opinion that meditation was very difficult and it required a great deal of hard work and many years of regular practice to get anywhere near success.

The novices and beginners had no real choice but to quietly listen to the discussion. After hearing the heated exchanges among their seniors, the novices got more confused and perplexed than ever. They were wondering whether it was a true *satsang* on meditation among spiritually enlightened people or just another debate among ordinary people over trivial matters. I also started wondering whether meditation was really all that difficult. If it was, why were they doing it for such a long time? Why didn't they just give it up? Why waste time? What must be their motivation?

It appeared to me that those who were doing meditation for a long time were very proud people. They were proud because they had been practising it for such a long time. As a silent observer and quiet listener, I thought that pride was always bad, whether it was about meditation or anything else. It appeared to me that gratification of the ego through pride was their prime motive. Their discussion continued for a long time, but it led them nowhere.

I also felt that none of those who were discussing this issue so vehemently had the slightest idea of how much harm their pride was doing to them. Pride can never do us any good – it only protects and nurtures the ego and keeps us removed from reality.

Ego and pride are fundamental facets. They make us do different things in order to create and reinforce our individual identity, which separates us from others. Everybody seeks respect from others. It is one of the most vital needs of human life. We all want social recognition and social sanction for whatever we are doing. Everybody wants to attract the attention of other people and prove that they are different. Attracting attention is an attempt on our part to prove that we are able to do things that others can't do.

When somebody does something that others cannot do, people begin to praise such a person. Naturally, he begins to feel proud of himself. If somebody is found to be practising meditation for a long time, everybody usually starts praising him. The person gets easily carried away by such praise and starts feeling proud about it.

One may think that having a small degree of pride is quite natural and is perfectly justified. However, we have to remember that although pride is very common, not everything that is common is necessarily desirable or appropriate – particularly when it is in the realm of spiritual practices.

Pride is eternally harmful for our spiritual progress. Even in small measures, it can contaminate the entire spectrum of our self-awareness and thus completely destroy our ability to reach higher spiritual experiences. Therefore, holding on to pride because it is considered natural is a self-defeating proposition.

Someone who has practised meditation for a long time may think that there is nothing wrong in feeling proud about something that they have been doing so persistently. They may also feel that it is quite natural. In spirituality, however, anything that restricts our perceptions and takes us away from reality is not worth striving for. Pride is harmful in this sense too.

Attracting Attention

It is true that meditation can sometimes seem difficult. It is bound to seem so because it is a special and unique kind of journey within us. This journey is completely different from the ones we are aware of. Therefore it is quite possible that initially one may get confused while walking on this path.

The real problem comes only when meditation is made to appear more difficult than it actually is – something that is often done to attract the attention of others and demand respect from them. Many people think that nobody is going to pay them any respect unless they do something extraordinary. They think they have to be different and so should be doing something very difficult – or at least it should appear so to others.

People who think like this may feel that if meditation appears easy to others and if anybody can do it, what differentiates them from other people? So they need to make it appear difficult. This is precisely what some spiritual leaders are doing and is the reason why meditation is made to look more difficult than it actually is.

Attention-seeking is not just a prerogative of spiritual leaders or practitioners of meditation. Many people do it for different reasons.

Mischievous children, college flirts, expensively dressed people at parties, worshippers performing complicated rituals and pseudo yogis standing on one foot or getting buried underground are all doing the same thing: attracting the attention of others.

It is said that the wheel that creates more noise gets oiled first. By the same token, unless you make some noise nobody is going to pay any special attention to you and your needs. But, in the process, you get caught up in the gimmicks to project a false picture and exploit the situation. A mischievous child exploits its mother by throwing emotional tantrums. A pseudo yogi and his fake devotees exploit the gullible and vulnerable. But gimmicks never work on a long-term basis. They get exposed sooner or later, so it is better to stay away from them and learn to differentiate between true and false. We need some time and patience to do that.

Exploiting Ignorance

Meditation is often made to look more difficult than it actually is because it provides an acceptable excuse in the event of possible failure. Such an excuse comes in handy for those who haven't achieved anything after years of practice. In this way they can safeguard their inflated self-images and explain their failure. It is very easy to conveniently blame the arduousness of the technique of meditation in order to defend their individual or collective failures.

It is quite understandable that some disciples are likely to find meditation more difficult than others, depending on their level of sincerity, regularity of practice and inherent ability.

So-called experts in all walks of life exploit people's ignorance and make themselves seem more important. For example, unprincipled garage mechanics might charge for work on your car that hasn't been done or doesn't need doing; corrupt officials might exploit those who are not aware of the formal government procedures; lawyers might exploit their clients by making legal procedures appear more complicated than they actually are.

Keeping it Covered Up

When it comes to meditation, exploitation is relatively easy. Whatever is said, done or experienced in relation to meditation is extremely subjective in nature, which makes it very difficult to be challenged by other people. It would be very difficult or almost impossible to disprove the claims made by someone who says that they had been practising meditation for many years.

There aren't any established or recognized parameters that can be used to prove or disprove such claims. Reduction in blood pressure, fall in pulse rate, increase in skin resistance, fall in blood lactate level and the presence of alpha waves on an electro-encephalogram are some of the indicators that could be used to assess these claims, but it is not practical to conduct such tests in everyday life. Unscrupulous people can very easily exploit such situations and bring disrepute to the field.

Everybody knows that getting the blood group and genetic constitution of a couple checked before they decide to get married can substantially reduce the chances of them having children with congenital and hereditary disorders. However, it is difficult to imagine people sharing their health files before falling in love with each other. In practice, it seems like an impossible proposition.

In India, there are people who privately are in favour and publicly are against the tradition of dowry. Dowry means a gift from the bride's parents to the bridegroom. Giving such gifts was understandable in the past, because in those days child marriages were quite prevalent in India.

In those days dowry was given out of natural love and affection for the bridegroom and his family. But later the tradition became a nuisance and a cause of serious anxiety to the bridal parents. It became obligatory and binding on them to give as much money as demanded by the in-laws.

Now, this particular practice has lost all its traditional beauty, meaning and relevance. In recent times, there have been several reported instances of lethal attacks being inflicted on young girls because they were unable to bring the outrageous amounts of money demanded by their in-laws. Of late, due to such atrocities, public awareness against dowry is growing.

However, the tradition has not been completely eradicated as yet. In actual practice, money still changes hands during marriages. The parents of the bride keep giving money to the bridegroom's parents who keep receiving it happily. In most cases, both choose to keep quiet about such transactions. Naturally, nobody knows what happens behind the scenes and the tradition continues unabated from one generation to another.

Something similar happens in the case of those who are teaching meditation and those who are being taught. Being truly successful in meditation is a long-term proposition. One has to spend many years to develop real mastery in meditation. It is quite difficult for most teachers and pupils to muster such long-term commitment to the cause of teaching or learning meditation. Consequently, they either resort to taking shortcuts or start projecting themselves as more superior than they actually are. In both situations, failure is almost certain in the end.

For any teacher, it is very embarrassing to concede failure in imparting proper knowledge to their pupils. It is equally embarrassing for a pupil to admit that he could not achieve anything substantial in meditation, even after years of regular practice.

If they both decide to keep quiet about their individual failures, nobody will ever come to know the truth. That is what most teachers and pupils appear to be doing. A sense of secrecy is constantly nurtured around the traditional relationship between a guru and his disciples. Everything that is spiritual is traditionally kept shrouded in mystery. Both teacher and pupil keep their ignorance and failure securely covered under the colourful garb of tradition. Ultimately they end up fooling themselves and others who come to learn meditation from them.

Under the leadership of such gurus and their disciples, different traditions of meditation manage to survive for some time and also grow to some extent. But sooner or later they tend to wither away because they usually lack substance.

A Clean Slate is Much Better
In my experience it is much easier to teach meditation to those who know nothing about it, than the ones who think that they know

everything. Those who want to learn it afresh carry a clean 'slate of mind' with them. Clean minds are far more receptive to learning than the ones that are full of information.

In contrast, those who are learned and have been practising meditation for a long time, or those who know a lot about it, are usually very rigid in their attitude towards learning. They are hardly receptive to anything new or different from what they already know or believe. This is particularly true of the long-term practitioners of meditation who have not taken the totality of yoga into account. Totality of yoga means its all-embracing, holistic perspective that encompasses individual and collective health and wellbeing. Mostly, they are not aware of all this and therefore carry a lot of misconceptions; they nurture wrong ideas and may have some idiosyncrasies about particular forms of meditation. They may be prejudiced in favour of one or against other forms of meditation.

Unless they are free of this burden, they cannot learn meditation properly. Teaching meditation to such people is a painstaking, time-consuming and mammoth task. It is like getting directly involved in a decoding process for which they are neither ready nor receptive. In effect, all the wrong impressions about the form of meditation they have been practising do not get properly resolved because they are not willing to be open to learn something completely new. It can therefore be a total waste of time. If it is not done properly, the burden of misconceptions continues. Ultimately, the pressure mounts so much that true learning and true teaching become impossible.

Some practitioners of meditation are dry, lifeless and closed. It is extremely difficult for them to accept that what they have been doing for all those years was wrong. Their inflated egos get in the way. In contrast, people who are leading ordinary lives make far better students. They know that they do not know anything about meditation and therefore they are keen to learn. It is said that you can wake up a person who is fast asleep if he is willing to wake up. But you cannot wake up somebody who is not willing to wake up. Similarly, one who wants to be a student and learn can be taught. But nobody can help a person who is happy in the deep slumber of ignorance and is reluctant to wake up.

SECRET NUMBER THREE

Know What Meditation is

1

Meditation – A Natural State of Being

In the previous chapter we saw that meditation is not really difficult, but it is often made to appear difficult by those who have vested interests in making it look harder to attain and by those who are more interested in exploiting others than in teaching.

Unnatural is Natural

Meditation is likely to be difficult for those who have a tendency to take everything too seriously, and for those who have only a superficial interest in it. It may also be difficult for those who are not doing it properly.

In reality, meditation is the most simple thing in the world. It should in fact be a natural state for us. It is the very essence of our core being. Initially, one finds it hard to believe that meditation could be so simple.

We find it difficult only because our everyday life has become too complex. Our routines, lifestyle and thinking have become extremely artificial, complicated and contaminated at all levels. Under the influence of such contamination, we seem to have forgotten the wonderful naturalness that came with us when we were born. This naturalness has been with us ever since, but unfortunately whatever we have learned after birth has become more important to us. Artificiality has become our way of life. It is as if 'unnaturalness' has become more natural to us than real 'naturalness'.

That is why meditation, which in fact should be natural and easy for us, has become more difficult and more complex. The thing which should be closest to us is farthest away.

Familiarity Breeds Contempt

The people closest to us play an important role in our life. They contribute a great deal to making our life rich and meaningful. But they are often so close to us that we usually tend to take them for granted. Most of us don't even appreciate or readily acknowledge their valuable contribution to our life. Children seldom see their parents as people who wish them well, often because they are too close to them.

Often children do not understand the real meaning and intention behind the instructions given by their parents and like to rebel by doing exactly the opposite. They get a kick out of such reactionary behaviour. It is very strange that children usually refuse to take any assistance or guidance from their parents when they really need it most and when their parents are also willing to go out of their way to give it to them.

Teenagers often may go through a very crucial and trying phase known as an 'identity crisis'. During this delicate period, they are in search of their own individuality. They prefer to stay away from parental influence, because they like to explore and experiment with their life all by themselves or with the help of their peers. Sometimes they cut themselves off from their parents, often showing a lack of respect, let alone taking any help from them.

There is nothing wrong in trying to establish one's individual identity, as long as it is done properly. But most teenagers tend to do it at the cost of helpful advice they could have easily had from their 'worldly wise' parents. As a result, youngsters have to go through a lot of unnecessary toil to establish themselves. In the process, they often pay a heavy price to gain first-hand experience of worldly matters. They are in fact, supposed to 'sit on the shoulders' of their parents to get a wider vision of life. They may deny that this is an advantage, but they need to do this to get a proper view of life around them. However, they spend a lot of time and energy looking for an alternative method to attain the same thing.

Something similar happens in the case of meditation. The state of meditation is really very close to us right from our birth. It is even closer than our parents are. In fact, meditation is the closest thing to us.

Our mind is a tool we use for establishing a connection with the external world. Whenever we get connected with something in the world around us, we move away from our true self. We also relate to the outer world through our actions, thoughts and emotions. During deep meditation, all our physical, mental and emotional activities come to a complete standstill. When our body, mind and emotions are absolutely still, we are in tune and in harmony with our true self. Being one with our true self is what we achieve through meditation.

We have to make a special effort to get connected with our true self through meditation, because we have lost touch with it. Our mind and thoughts influence our life so much that we cannot conceive of anything beyond our mind. Our thoughts should really be more distant and foreign to us than our true self. It is because our thinking faculty develops much later after our birth. When we came into this world this faculty was present in us, but it was in a rudimentary form. In the early stages of our life we carry some images or pre-thoughts, but they are not fully developed.

At birth, as we were in a thought-free state, we were at one with our true self. Being at one with our true self was like being in a state of bliss. Thinking is an acquired skill which develops later, but a thought-free state is our true nature. Therefore, meditation, in which our mind is completely free of thoughts, should really be a very natural experience to us. We don't realize this, because we are very close to our true self – our extreme closeness to it makes it harder to see.

Because of this closeness, we start taking our true self for granted. It is also interesting to see how we take all our body organs for granted and do not pay adequate attention to their health and wellbeing. A time comes when they start developing problems and suddenly we become aware of their presence. When we suffer from a splitting headache, we acknowledge the existence of a body part called the head. Similarly, if there is a pain in the chest we suddenly realize that we have a chest. We don't feel the need to remember that they are parts of our body, as long as there aren't any problems with those organs. That is why we usually forget to acknowledge and respect their deserved place of true importance in our life.

In the same manner, when children are grown up they conveniently forget about the caring attention they received from their parents and the hardships their parents had to go through while bringing them up. It is therefore advisable to send our children away for some time every year to a relative or friend's house or maybe to a school in another part of the country. Occasional exposure to an outside environment goes a long way. It has a tremendous educational value. After exposure to the outside world, children begin to understand and appreciate the real worth of parental love.

It is There within Us

Something similar happens in the case of meditation as well. We do not understand its real worth until we have gone a long way away from it, away from our true self.

We go through a lot of hardships and toiling trying to be happy in worldly life. After spending half our lives in this manner, we suddenly recognize that the kind of 'happiness' we actually have is not what we were looking for. Realization dawns upon us that worldly happiness cannot fill the void we have within us. Eventually, we get thoroughly exhausted and disillusioned with running after such happiness. Then the real exploration of our inner world begins. Meditation provides proper direction to this exploration, which ultimately takes us to the inner reservoir of happiness.

It is one of the greatest revelations to realize that the happiness we were searching for in the external world always existed within us.

After such a revelation, all ambiguity about meditation disappears and we begin to understand that meditation is not very difficult. We subsequently make good progress in meditation.

2

What Is Meditation?

So far we have discussed some important issues related to meditation: issues like the importance of taking a broader view, knowing how it helps in solving our day-to-day problems, knowing what it is not, seeing that it is not very difficult and that it is not the privilege of a select few. Now, it is time to find out the exact meaning of meditation.

Meditation is a Thought-Free State of Mind

There are different definitions of meditation given by different people from across the subject, but the classic textbooks on yoga say that meditation means the perpetual dwelling of the mind on some object that subsequently fades into 'no-thing-ness'.

Meditation essentially means temporary freedom from thoughts. Unlike sleep, it is a 'wakeful' thought-free state, in which all our senses are alert and awake. In fact, during meditation, we are many times more alert and awake than during our day-to-day life. It is a state of mind in which our thinking process stops for a short period of time. During meditation, one experiences a complete stillness of the mind, great serenity, dynamic stability and profound quietude.

Do Not Use Force

Often after starting meditation practice, we feel desperate to experience peace of mind. Consequently, we may feel like driving all the disturbing thoughts out of our mind.

More often than not, such desperate attempts towards appeasement of the mind prove futile. We never find lasting success through such endeavours. Nothing is really achieved through 'force'. Those who try to force it will never be able to meditate properly and therefore will never experience true peace of mind.

To push aside thoughts arising in the mind is by itself the wrong way to meditate. It is as absurd as trying to purify muddy water by hand picking the clay particles suspended in it. We may spend many, many hours, days and months doing this exercise, but nothing will happen. The muddy water will remain as muddy as ever. It will never become clear. In fact, it will become muddier than before.

What we need to do is to just keep the vessel containing such turbid water to one side and patiently wait for the water to become clearer. After some time, we will find that the suspended clay particles slowly settle down to the bottom of the vessel on their own and the water is becoming clearer. Being hasty in such matters is seldom fruitful. In fact it is counterproductive.

What is true with muddy water is equally true with our mind. It cannot be made silent with the help of our purposeful efforts to silence it. If we apply force, it will become more agitated and restless. Instead, if we allow our mind to get settled naturally – if we do not control our thoughts; if we do not interfere with its operations – it will become quiet more readily.

Do Not Avoid Thoughts

Ramakrishna Paramahansa was one of the greatest sages. A *sadhaka* once went to see him to seek his guidance on how to make better progress in meditation. He complained that his mind was never free of thoughts, in spite of his persistent efforts to silence it. After understanding what type of meditation the *sadhaka* was practising, Ramakrishna suggested he continue with his meditation as usual, except that he should avoid all thoughts about monkeys during meditation. Ramakrishna asked him to come back after a week to report on his progress.

After eight days, when he came to see Ramakrishna the *sadhaka* looked very upset. He complained to the master, 'Oh Great Master, what have you done to me? I have been doing meditation for the past several years, and the thought of monkeys never touched my mind during meditation. But since you told me not to think of monkeys, my mind is constantly flooded with thoughts about monkeys! I am constantly stressed that I should not be letting the thoughts of monkey come into my mind! Now I am so obsessed about not having any thoughts about monkeys, that I feel very restless. I am not able to eat or sleep properly. I don't know what to do. I am totally confused and frustrated. When I approached you a week ago, I thought that, with your counsel, I would be able to meditate better. Forget doing it better – I can't even meditate for a minute now. All the time, there is an apprehension that the thought of monkeys will come into my mind. Instead of becoming more silent, my mind is getting more and more agitated. There are monkeys jumping all the time, all over the place in my mind, doing all kinds of tricks. Now, my mind is more restless than ever before. I have completely lost peace of mind.'

After listening compassionately to the sad predicament of the *sadhaka*, Ramakrishna clarified everything. 'I am sorry for all the suffering you had to go through during last week. But I had no better way to make my point clear to you more effectively. My intention was not to disturb or trouble you at all. Believe me, I only wanted to help you. After one week of trial, now you know through your personal experience that the more you try to avoid something, the more difficult it becomes to stay away from it! For the whole week, all the time, you tried your best to prevent any thoughts about monkeys from coming into your mind. But now you know what happens when you try too hard to avoid something. Therefore, my advice to you is that you should not try to avoid any thoughts, but just witness them all. If you follow this advice, you will certainly do well in meditation. Don't worry. My blessings are with you. I wish you all the best!'

We have to remember the message contained in this story. During meditation, we are not supposed to *make* our mind silent, but *let* it settle down on its own. We should also not try to push our thoughts aside, but make sure that they become silent on their own.

3

Study your Thoughts to
Go Beyond Them

An inevitable question that springs to mind is that if during meditation thoughts are allowed to come and go as they wish and if they are not restrained, will they not grow unhindered? Moreover, by assuming a passive approach, like a witness, are we not in effect fostering laziness and inactivity?

Remove the Causes of Restlessness
It is quite understandable that one may have such anxiety. Fortunately we don't have to worry about such untoward effects if we are practising meditation properly.

When we do not oppose or pursue our thoughts, they gradually reduce in intensity and number. Eventually, the very process of thinking comes to a complete standstill. This is the most fundamental process involved in meditation. We can only understand this through first-hand experience.

Meditation is not a matter of mere intellectual gymnastics, but a process of experiential understanding. We must therefore try to have a direct experience of this truth. That is, we have to start studying our thoughts to go beyond them.

Just sit quietly in one place and try to study and follow all your thoughts as and when they come to your mind. In the course of time, you will yourself begin to discover the truth. Once we realize from this experience that thinking gets activated only when we take interest in some thoughts and oppose others, the iron grip of thoughts on our mind begins to slacken. As soon as the influence of thoughts on our being is substantially reduced, the mind unwinds itself into a no-thought state. It is a peculiar state, which is altogether different in quality and character from all other states of consciousness that we are conscious of. While being in this state we are aware of all the mental activities, but do not respond to any one of them. We are supposed only to observe those activities in an 'unattached' manner. I purposely use the word 'unattached' in place of 'detached', because it has a more positive connotation to it.

The word 'unattached' implies more than 'detached'. It implies that it is our free choice not to get attached to our thoughts and that we are not afraid of them. We are keenly interested in knowing more about our mind through careful observation of its operations. These operations are perceived as a never-ending flow of thoughts. The thoughts keep appearing in the field of consciousness of our mind. Unlike 'detached', 'unattached' indicates a more positive state, where there is better understanding and more wisdom. The word 'detached' gives a feeling that we dislike our mind and that is why we want to stay away from our thoughts. It also implies that we are scared of our thoughts. But our mind can never be truly silent unless we approach it with a positive attitude to understand it better.

Over a period of time, our mind does become silent, but because we are fully aware of this silence, it never leads to inactivity or laziness. In fact, it greatly improves the overall quality of our self-awareness. Once the awareness is improved, there is no room left for any laziness or inactivity to creep in.

There is no point in spending our precious time in trying to make our mind silent. It will be much better if we understand the reasons for its restlessness and try to take proper care of those factors. Once we discover, understand and take care of all the factors that are responsible for our mental agitation and restlessness, it will be very easy to silence our mind.

Restlessness is the Very Nature of the Mind

When we start studying why our mind becomes restless, we realize that a continuous flow of thoughts makes it restless. We also realize that thinking and thoughts are the inherent characteristics of the human mind and restlessness is its very nature.

How can we get rid of the mind's intrinsic tendency to think? And if we make our mind lose its identity, can we call what is left behind 'mind'? Can a mind be separated from its thoughts? Can a flower and its fragrance, or a flower and its beauty be separated from each other? A flower, its beauty and its fragrance are the inseparable constituents of the same object called a flower. Its beauty and fragrance entirely depend on its existence as a flower. If we separate its beauty, can a flower remain as a flower?

It means that the flower's innate essence of being a flower goes hand in hand with its beauty and fragrance. It is equally true with tides in the ocean. If the tides are separated from the ocean, what is left behind is surely not an ocean. An ocean cannot survive in the absence of its waves.

Similarly, the mind's innate essence entirely depends on its thoughts. The mind cannot remain as the mind if there are no thoughts in it. It is impossible to separate the object from its inbuilt characteristics. If we try to do that, the object's 'objectness' is lost. That is why when the mind becomes free of its thoughts, it is no longer a mind. When the thoughts are erased, the mind is also automatically erased. This particular state is called 'no-mind state'.

Experience the True Self through Meditation

With the help of meditation, we have to first reach a state of 'no-thought awareness' and then make use of this state to come closer to our true self.

If we want to know what our true self is like, we have to do something to actually experience its presence within ourselves. But there isn't any direct way of knowing our true self. It is just not possible to do that. We have therefore to first find out what it is *not* and on the basis of this knowledge figure out what it actually *is*. This is called the process of elimination.

To arrive at a proper diagnosis, doctors often make use of this method. They begin with the careful study of the presenting symptoms of a patient. Then they shortlist the diseases which would cause patient to come in with these symptoms. After analysing the available information and after prudent clinical examination of the patient, the patient undergoes certain investigations.

After careful circumspection of the available information, doctors start using the process of elimination to come to a final conclusion about the diagnosis. During this process, they go on ruling out the possibility of one disease after another, until they arrive at a final diagnosis. Thus, the doctors first see what their patient is not suffering from to decide what he is suffering from.

The police follow the same procedure while investigating a crime. First, they consider all possibilities that might have led to the occurrence of a crime. Then in the light of all available information they shortlist the suspects who are likely to have had a motive to commit the crime. Through the process of elimination they finally reach the actual culprit.

We often use this process in our day-to-day life. When we do not have access to the full truth we have to resort to such indirect methods. The process of elimination helps us isolate 'cause' from 'effect'.

We have to use this method to eliminate what is not our true self in order to find our true self. To understand the true self, we first of all have to eliminate all that is 'not' real self, to gradually arrive at the experience of our real self. Once we have first-hand experience of our real self, we automatically develop a true taste for meditation. In due course, the influence of the real self on our life grows and the influence of thoughts slowly withers away. Thereafter, the reins of our life are transferred to the able hands of our true self, which begins to rule our life in a much better manner.

4

Meditation Should be Practised with Utmost Ease

So far we have seen that meditation is a self-induced state of thought-free wakefulness. There are two more important aspects to meditation. One is effortlessness and the other is inner joy.

Meditation is a spiritual practice or *sadhana*, which needs to be performed over a long period of time on a continual basis. We can do it on a long-term basis only if it is very easy to understand, simple to perform and effortless to practise. Moreover, it should bring joy into our life.

If the meditation we practise is as simple, effortless and natural as our normal breathing, it can be done with maximum ease. Such meditation can be easily practised on a regular basis.

Later on, we won't have to *do* it, it will just keep *happening*. We won't have to put in any conscious effort to get into a state of meditation. It becomes an integral part of our life, as if it is second nature. As we progress further on the path, it can even become first nature.

The important question here is: do we need to put in some effort to let our meditation become effortless and natural? If so, would it not affect the naturalness of meditation? Is it not paradoxical to put in effort to become effortless?

Living with Paradoxes

This is quite a pertinent question. It appears paradoxical but then life itself is a bundle of paradoxes. The greatest among them is the co-existence of two opposite concepts like life and death, the two fundamental states of existence. Life and death are so different from each other and yet they remain inseparably intertwined throughout our lives.

Apparently, our life begins at the time of our birth and ends when we die. During our present life itself we can experience various changes – the 'death' of our childhood, being 'reborn' as adolescents; the adolescent phase culminating into adulthood and so on, until we reach old age and finally die the death of our present body.

This means that the 'death' of one phase leads to the 'life' of another phase. This further means that life and death are intrinsically connected with each other. If the earlier phases of our 'life' transform into the later phases, can we really pinpoint where the earlier phase ends and the new phase begins? It is not possible, because the process of living and dying are intimately connected with each other.

The paradox of making use of effort to learn effortlessness is a very trivial paradox compared to the greatest paradox of the symbiosis of life and death. Interestingly, if we accept this fundamental paradox of life and learn to live with it, bringing effortlessness into our meditation becomes a very easy affair.

Effort is Needed in the Beginning

In the initial stages, when we are just beginning to learn and practise meditation, we have to make some effort. It is like learning to ride a bicycle. Initially, as novices, we have to pay equal attention to the brakes, pedals and the road on which we are riding the bike. When we start pedalling, we lose track of the brakes. If we pay extra attention to the brakes, we tend to forget the orientation of the road. We start paying attention to the road and forget to apply the brakes. We fall off the bike and get hurt. By the time one wound heals, another follows.

If we are able to weather this storm, persevere and keep learning, after a few days we develop mastery over bicycle riding. Then we can ride it fast or slow, try acrobatics like riding without holding the handle, chat with a friend who is riding by our side, or look around once in a while rather than focusing on the road all the time. We do not usually meet with an accident in spite of all the gymnastics, because of our expertise in riding a bike. We don't need to exert ourselves too much; riding becomes more and more effortless and smooth.

While we are learning a new skill, we have to put in some effort. But, as learning approaches completion, the amount of effort we need to put in decreases. As we get more and more proficient in a new skill we can do it with less effort.

Something similar happens when we start learning meditation. In the beginning, we have to be very particular about where we do it, at what time, and what sort of mood we are in. We have to do it regularly. If we continue with grit, determination and perseverance, we develop in meditation. Gradually, it becomes more and more effortless. After more practice and perfection, we don't have to be so particular about the place, time or other small details. We are still able to reach the effortless and thought-free state that we are supposed to reach through meditation, but without much extraneous help. This is what is supposed to happen if we are really on the right path.

Don't Give Excessive Importance to Extraneous Factors

It is true that, to a certain extent, external help is necessary, particularly when one is a novice in meditation. But we need not be too fussy about these things. We must never let secondary factors become more important than the actual meditation. Otherwise, we may just get stuck in rituals and waste our time in doing things of lesser importance.

A properly worked out regime regarding time, place, etc. certainly helps in becoming mentally silent and free of thoughts in a shorter time. However, if our mind doesn't become silent in spite of such discipline, it obviously means that our main objective is not being achieved. In that situation, all the drill that we have been doing in the name of meditation becomes a meaningless and wasteful activity. Therefore, one should not be too finicky about the extraneous factors.

Many *sadhakas* tend to miss this vital point and give excessive importance to trivial matters, losing sight of the main goal of meditation.

Whereas those who have mastered the art of meditation never give undue prominence to the unimportant things. They know exactly what role the external factors play in their *sadhana*.

Why People Become Fussy

Those who do not understand the essence of meditation, in spite of strict discipline and regular practice, tend to deviate from the main path. The rituals become more important to them than the actual meditation. It is very interesting to understand the psychological factors responsible for such behaviour. Most of those who highlight rituals do so because they want to augment their own importance under the guise of such rituals.

These are the people who have not made much headway in meditation or have failed to develop a true taste for meditation in spite of their persistent efforts. They find it hard to digest failure and therefore get very frustrated. Sometimes, the fear of failure is so strong that they are even scared of making any efforts to overcome such failure. Things become even worse if they stop putting in the effort. They start seeking easy escapes. Over a period of time, the trivial things related to meditation become more important than the actual meditation.

Aping the Spiritual Masters

The inner state of meditation reached by a spiritual master is beyond the comprehension of most people. Everyone is, however, attracted towards the serene, peaceful, joyous, caring, cheerful and loving disposition of the master, and may feel tempted to imitate the maestro.

It is relatively easy to simulate the master at a physical, superficial level, but quite hard to go through the entire process of spiritual evolution to reach the same level of consciousness. It is easy to blindly follow a master, to glorify him and his teachings, but not so easy to comprehend the reality and live with such a realization.

By merely looking at the external appearance of Lord Buddha sitting in a lotus pose under a tree, it is not possible to exactly perceive his inner state of meditation. There is no way to know what is happening inside him and what is he experiencing within himself. It is easy to sit under a similar tree in a lotus pose with back straight and eyes closed *like* Buddha, than to actually *be* a Buddha.

Nothing significant happens in a person who is doing this kind of imitation for a long time. By mere physical simulation, how can one change from within? One is bound to remain as miserable and restless as one was before the imitation. When nothing happens after a period of time, one begins to lose patience. But in the absence of an alternative, people often prefer to continue aping the master.

Inability to Differentiate between Means and an End

By merely sitting erect and steady in a lotus pose, or by wearing a gentle smile on the face like Buddha, one may experience a momentary calmness of mind, but this does not bring lasting peace of mind and bliss.

One cannot experience the real state of meditation by merely sitting in a perfect lotus pose for several hours. Although, as we make progress in meditation, we can sit in one position for many hours at a stretch, which is what Buddha actually did. Merely putting on a smiling face like Buddha, however, is not going to bring any real success in meditation.

The face automatically lights up with a radiant smile if there is real joy and bliss inside. The inner state of joy is reflected on the face. We don't have to do anything special.

Experiencing inner joy can be a long process. Very few people have enough patience or perseverance to start the process and take it to completion. Inevitably, one gets drawn towards less important issues related to meditation and starts attaching unnecessary significance to them. Eventually, one loses sight of the actual goal of one's *sadhana*. As a result, trivia become more important than matters of real significance.

5

Being in a Meditative State
is our Very Nature

Ease of Breathing

Although the practice of meditation initially demands effort, eventually it becomes our nature. We can continue to stay in a state of meditation while we are sitting or walking, eating or drinking, sleeping or wide awake, talking or being quiet. Meditation becomes an effortless perpetual state. Just like breathing, meditation goes on all the time with ease and naturalness.

We are able to breathe because we are alive. All our muscles of respiration, lungs and ribs would be useless for breathing if there is no life in our body. It is wrong to say that we are alive because of our breathing and we die when our breathing stops. When breathing and pulse stop, doctors declare that someone is dead. In reality, the reverse is true: we are not alive because of our breathing – because we are alive, we are able to breathe.

One may argue that if breathing continues because we are alive, we should be able to hold our breath for any length of time at will. But our experience contradicts that. If we stop breathing even for a few seconds, we experience an unbearable uneasiness and feel as if our life is being snuffed out. Why should this happen? The answer is that trying to stop breathing obstructs the mechanism that is designed to keep us alive. Our life principle activates as a part of its efforts to protect us from dying. Thus, it compels us to exhale or inhale depending on where in the breathing cycle we had stopped our breathing.

Life Principle Gives Vitality to Breathing

There is no doubt that breathing is helpful to the life principle, but it is not quite right to say that breathing gives life to the life principle.

It is true that a farmer ploughs the field, sows the seeds, puts in fertilizers, removes weeds, tends the land and in the end, reaps the harvest. But he cannot be considered as the 'originator' of the incredible capacity of land to produce many grains from a single seed. What he does is only to make an intelligent use of nature's capacity to create, in order to get a good yield from his land.

He nurtures the crop by using fertilizers, but that doesn't mean that he is the 'creator' of the 'nourishing power' of the fertilizers. The nourishing power is a gift of nature. The farmer just uses this potential to his advantage, but that does not make him the owner of this potential.

First Step Determines the Direction

While undertaking any journey, the first step we take is very important. It determines the direction and entire course of the journey that follows. If the first step is taken in the right direction, the rest of the steps will usually automatically follow suit. A farmer can get a good harvest provided he makes the right selection of seeds to be sown in his land. If the initial selection is wrong, the chances of having a good harvest become too slim to justify the effort. How he makes the original selection determines the future of the crop he is going to harvest.

Like a farmer, we have to be careful when making the choice of meditation we propose to learn and practise, before we can expect to reap the harvest of inner joy and lasting peace of mind. To have a genuine urge to learn meditation is in itself a rarity, particularly when it is learned for the joy of learning and not merely for the cure of some physical, psychological or psychosomatic health problem. Once the journey of meditation is properly begun, the rest of the voyage becomes joyful automatically. Moreover, if the ultimate goal of our meditation is to become one with the universal cosmic consciousness, we have to find some early signs of such a momentous objective in the very first step we take in that direction. If we develop effortless ease through meditation, it paves the way to glimpsing our real self, which is pure individual consciousness – the reflection of universal cosmic consciousness.

In the same manner, if effortlessness is the final objective of our meditation, it should be present right from the very first step we take on the path. If there is unnaturalness in our meditation when we start doing it for the first time, the same unnaturalness may continue in our practice for a long time. Later, it is very difficult to bring natural effortlessness back to our meditation practice.

The meditation we want to practice should have the necessary potential to be an integral part of our life. We should not have to put in extra effort for that at a later stage.

Meditation Should be a Simple and Easy Journey

Which particular type of meditation we want to practise is not so important, but it is vital that it is easy and simple to learn and practise. It is better to be vigilant about this point before we begin.

During any journey, we have to ensure from time to time that we are going in the right direction. For that, we have to look at the milestones, get proper directions from an experienced person who has been to our destination before and, once in a while, also refer to a map for confirmation. In the same manner, we have to take proper 'directions' or guidance about meditation from an experienced yogi before we start our journey of meditation. After starting meditation, we have to seek counsel from time to time, to confirm that we are moving in the right direction. We have to also look for the 'milestones' or the signs of progress we have made on the path, such as developing a feeling of wellbeing, improving peace of mind, decreasing irritability, improving relations with others and so on. It is also necessary to compare notes with fellow travellers and refer to the 'map' of spiritual evolution described in the scriptures on yoga, to ensure that everything is moving smoothly.

We have to also pay careful attention to whether meditation is becoming second nature to us or not – whether we tend to forget about meditation during the course of the day or remember it all the time. Whether we have to struggle to bring back our attention to meditation, or whether we do it with great joy and ease. It is obvious that whatever is easy and simple to do is easy to remember too. In contrast, anything that is difficult to perform is difficult to remember.

Looking after a child is a 'job' for a babysitter, but more natural for its mother, as she is instinctively committed to the welfare of her child. Meditation is simple and easy to those who are committed to self-knowledge. Doing well in meditation means achieving holistic growth in life.

6

The Body is the House,
the Life Principle its Owner

We have to keep in mind that consciousness, or the life principle within us, is the real owner of our life. Only by its decree do we live in our body. Its presence within us is essential to perform the activities that we do while we are alive. The house of our body is meant for and belongs to this principle. Our bodily existence in this world solely depends upon the existence and sanction of this owner. Whenever we forget this fundamental reality we have to face problems in our life.

We have to get reintroduced to the owner through our meditation. I have purposely used the word 'reintroduce', because the majority of us are not aware of the basis of our existence. We have to recognize the existence of this living force within us with absolute clarity and certainty. Once we do that, our life is automatically filled with peace, energy and vigour.

Once our acquaintance with the life principle is re-established, we automatically become one with this energy. After such oneness, whatever we do in life becomes so much better than what we have done before. Once we are one with the life principle, it brings a marked qualitative improvement in our life.

Permission to Use is Not Ownership
We all know that during the presidential term, the US president lives in the White House and the Prime Minister of Great Britain lives at 10 Downing Street in London. After the presidential tenure is over,

though, the president has to vacate the White House, whether they like it or not. It is quite possible that the president, after a few years in the White House, may feel that the premises belong to him and that he is the actual owner of the place. However, this would not change the reality. Once his term is over, he will realize who the real owner is. Sometimes tenants living in a rented house begin to think that they own the property, particularly when the owner doesn't come forward to establish ownership rights.

Something similar happens in the case of the life principle within us. The life principle, the real owner of our body, never comes forward to establish its ownership, so we tend to conveniently overlook its existence and assume that we are the real owner.

7

Meditation Should Bring Joy

In addition to freedom from thoughts, effortlessness and attentiveness, joy should also be an essential and integral part of our meditation. However, if we crave such joy through our meditation, it will never come to us. In fact, such craving can actually disturb and distract us so much that it will be very difficult to meditate properly and with ease.

After we have truly mastered the art of meditation and are able to meditate in an effortless manner, we discover the ever-present ocean of happiness within us. We start bathing in this ocean of joy and experience the delight of floating in the never-ending tides of bliss.

It is truly a great revelation to understand that if we chase after joy it will elude us, but the moment we stop such efforts, joy will start flowing over us in abundance.

High Quality Work is Essential for Affluence and Wealth

In India, traditionally Lakshmi is worshipped as the goddess of wealth. It is said that the goddess of wealth blesses those who are focused on doing their assigned work with exquisite quality and dedication, not those who are desperately running after her. This is equally applicable in the case of joy. We have to carefully understand the deeper meaning of this saying about wealth. If we are not chasing after money, but are in search of excellence in the work we are doing with great dedication, the goddess of wealth will be very pleased with our work. Naturally she will feel like being with us, which means we will make a lot of money because of our high-quality, dedicated work. However, if we are obsessed about making a lot of money and think about nothing else but money all day, the quality of our work will suffer and the goddess of wealth is bound to run away from us.

If our only concern in life is money, then we will always be pondering over profits and the ways and means of increasing our profits. This will distract our attention from achieving excellence and perfection in our work. Consequently, the quality of the work we are doing and the product we are selling in the market will both suffer. Obviously, with deteriorating quality, the demand for our product in the market will decline. We will soon start losing our share and reputation in the market. The sales of our product will start going down. Our business profits will also drop. Naturally, we will make less money.

In contrast, if we are vigilant and watchful about achieving excellence in our work and are completely dedicated to it, the quality of our work will keep improving substantially. If 'total customer satisfaction' is our top priority in business, we will make maximum effort to see to it that our customers are happy with our product and remain so. For that to happen, we will keep on improving the quality of our product. Consequently, demand for our products will continue to rise. The number of satisfied customers who look forward to buying our products will also keep growing. Naturally, our business will grow in leaps and bounds. Money and prosperity will soon start coming to us in abundance.

Excellence in Meditation Leads to Joy

These principles of excellence can equally be applied to the 'spiritual wealth' we acquire through meditation. Proper practice of meditation with full dedication, perseverance and perfection, can bring inner joy and lasting peace, which is the real 'spiritual wealth' that comes as a by-product of our meditation practice.

While working in the field of yoga, I come across different kinds of people. Some of them would say that, despite their best efforts, they were not able to meditate properly. Others said that they could meditate, but never experienced the inner joy that I was talking about.

All of them struggled in their practices of meditation. They made the whole process of meditation too laborious. They were constantly haunted by the thought of experiencing inner joy and bliss – but such obsession itself precludes them from getting what they are looking for.

People who say that they can meditate but are not able to derive any joy from it, are basically doing it wrong somehow. Either the method of meditation they are following is wrong for them or the guidance they are getting about meditation is wrong. If you are practising meditation correctly, it should bring boundless inner joy, which is the most natural and spontaneous outcome of meditation. Ecstasy is an innate characteristic of meditation.

8

Meditation – The Divine Play

Balance between Being Worldly and Being Spiritual

At times, after I have finished a lecture on meditation, somebody from the audience, curious to know more about it, often asks a very interesting and amusing question: 'Dr Vinod, how long have you been on the path of emancipation?' I always wonder why anybody would ask such a question.

Those who ask this question are usually good people – they do not mean anything bad by it. They are deeply interested in knowing more about meditation and other important issues related to spiritual way of living. But from the manner in which they ask this question it appears that they are trying to separate the spiritual from the earthly life.

There are many reasons why one might ask this question. One is that they might think that the path of meditation is the same as the path of emancipation. No doubt they are related to each other, but the people who ask this question are usually trying to separate meditation from worldly life.

Or they might believe that one who takes to meditation must be doing it for a reason: maybe a sick person who is trying to escape from worldly problems by taking recourse to meditation, or seeking liberation from the birth and death cycles. Or they might assume that by being on the path of meditation one would leave their family, friends and relatives behind, becoming a recluse, and leading a secluded life away from society. This is a mistaken notion that emancipation demands dissociation from worldly life and involves giving up material pleasures. Some might equate the path of meditation with the path of emancipation. Some might think that wearing saffron robes and putting a serious expression on your face are the only qualifications needed to be a spiritual person. They don't know that meditation brings harmony between our material and spiritual life and, in due time, it becomes inseparably integrated with our daily living.

Taking Meditation Too Seriously or Too Lightly

Once, I was addressing a gathering of regular practitioners of meditation. They all looked so serious and wore such long faces that for one moment I sincerely thought that there must have been some serious mishap or death in the near relatives of one of the members of the group. Most people believe that meditation is a very serious affair and we must put on a grim face while doing it. There are also people who look at meditation as a kind of entertainment and as such tend to take it too lightly. However, if we want to take meditation to fruition, we should neither take it too seriously nor too lightly.

After regular practice of meditation our life will be filled with abundant joy and profound peace. It is, however, very difficult to maintain such regularity if we treat meditation as a matter of duty and not as a matter of sport which is to be played for the pure joy and recreation of it. Being playful is a matter of attitude.

Unfortunately, very few practitioners approach meditation in a playful way. Most of them are far too serious about it. That is why, in spite of many years of practice, they do not experience any joy. There are hardly any visible signs of joy in their life; rather, they look very sad and tense, with deep furrows on their foreheads.

Meditation is unquestionably a unique kind of game. We have to play this game on our home ground – that is, within ourselves. To play this special game we don't have to go anywhere, because the play, the player, the playground and the equipment are all readily available within us.

Once we develop enough proficiency in this game, we begin to derive lot of fun and joy from it. It is a special kind of joy which comes from within. The joy of meditation is vastly different from all other types of joy that we are aware of. It is the joy of being in our own company.

Inner joy is completely independent of the moods and vagaries of the outer world. It truly makes us self-sufficient.

We don't have to break away from the outer world to reach there. Once we are spiritually evolved, it is possible to remain well-grounded within ourselves all the time, without getting perturbed by the ever-changing external world. I was very fortunate to be able to enjoy meditation immensely right from day one. I have now been enjoying it for more than 35 years.

In short, we may say that there are two types of people who take to meditation in the wrong way: those who embrace it with undue seriousness and those who treat it in a casual manner. Both are mistaken, because meditation is to be done neither too seriously nor too lightly. Both miss the point and therefore do not get anywhere, in spite of their efforts.

True Player and True Sportsman Spirit

A true player with a highly developed spirit of sportsmanship can easily understand the difference between taking something too seriously and taking it too lightly. No matter which game he/she is playing – it could be tennis, basketball or any other game – a true sportsperson is always able to draw a line between these two extremes.

He/she knows how to take success as well as failure in his/her stride and to learn from them both. He puts in all the effort to improve his performance and excel in the game. While doing so, his primary focus is never on mere performance, but on the immense joy he gets while playing the game to the best of his abilities.

To experience the immensity of this joy is the real motivating force behind all his efforts. He plays for the joy of playing. He likes to work hard to improve his performance in the game, because, by doing so, he is able to enjoy it better. Over a period of time, the sportsmanship spirit becomes an integral part of his being. It gets reflected in whatever he does in his daily life.

If somebody starts making fun of a true sportsman, or starts teasing or pulling his leg, he does not get upset about such insults and abuses, as long as they are done in good spirit. While playing, if he gets hurt, he does not make a big fuss about the injury. If the injury permits and the situation demands it, he continues to play, despite the pain.

Those who have a highly developed sportsman spirit are co-operative with others in a very natural and spontaneous manner. Being so, they enrich themselves and preserve their high spirits without any difficulty. Naturally, they are always at ease with themselves and others. After the contest is over, a true sportsman can sit with his opponent and have a friendly chat with him. Over a period of time, all such players become happy and peaceful. They soon get filled to the brim with immense joy and happiness.

When I refer to players, I do not necessarily mean just the successful players. Successful players are not always playful in their attitude and spirits; and those who are playful may not necessarily be successful in the conventional sense. Being successful in life is one thing and being successful in a game is another. Being successful in life means being truly happy, contented and peaceful, regardless of whether you are doing well in the game of life or not. A truly successful person is by and large a very playful person.

A successful player is highly competitive while he is playing the game. But, often he unconsciously carries this competitiveness into his personal life and therefore can never be truly happy and at peace with himself. If a competitive game and the competitive spirit are stretched beyond limits, they lead to unbearable stress and tension, which make the person miserable and unhappy. Any person who is under stress invites lot of suffering. When I refer to a play and players, I do not mean fiercely competitive games or highly competitive players. I am also not referring to those who are a big success or a big failure in any particular sport.

We have to make use of the game we are playing as a tool to develop good sportsmanship and then employ it to improve our performance in the game. While improving our performance, we must focus on enjoying the game rather than improving performance *per se*. Improvement in our performance is directly proportional to how much we enjoy playing the game and keep learning from it.

True sportsmanship leads to playfulness. Playfulness improves the quality of our understanding of the subtle points of the game. Proper understanding improves performance. Improved performance adds to the joy one derives from the game. The joy of the game permeates into the deeper parts of our being and thus gets integrated into the very fabric of our life.

Being Playful in Meditation

If we learn to look at meditation in the same playful manner as we do in the sport we play, we will be well on our way to becoming a happier person. Thereafter, the practice of meditation becomes more like fun than mere ritual.

If on a particular day, for some reason, we do not get the same joy from meditation as we did on the previous day, we do not get upset. Rather, we readily accept the incidental failure with grace and ease. Of course we have to be well grounded in our playful attitude towards meditation to make this happen.

In due course, the playful attitude becomes part of us. With the help of such an attitude, we can handle all the problems related to our inner world much more freely, boldly and squarely. Thus, problems get resolved more readily than ever before.

This playful attitude comes in handy when our mind gets over-crowded with different kinds of thoughts during meditation. We can look at those thoughts in a more cheerful manner, treat them as a part of the game of meditation and not let them upset us.

To do well in meditation, we have to be mentally prepared for a very long journey. During any long journey – particularly when it is a special kind of journey like meditation – we may have to go through some difficult, trying and disheartening times. When experiencing this, one may feel that it is the end of everything: it is like a 'black night of the soul'. Nothing seems to work for us anymore when we are in such a state. The gloomy, desolate feelings engulf us and our meditation does not work well in spite of our persistent efforts. It is like being in an unfathomable void of frustration and disappointment.

We may also feel that nothing has worked at all so far and that we are back to square one. We may even feel like questioning the very credibility and reliability of meditation. Many people who regularly practise meditation have to go through this painful experience at one time or another. It often comes to us when we least expect it and are hardly prepared for it. In particular, it happens to those who are taking meditation too seriously.

Those who take meditation too lightly don't go through such an ordeal, but they don't make much progress either. If the absence of problems goes hand in hand with lack of progress in meditation then such freedom from problems is of very little value. Life involves problems and our growth means we have to solve those problems. 'Growth with problems' is a better and more welcome option than 'no growth with no problems' as the alternative.

Right from the beginning, if we cultivate a playful attitude towards meditation, we will certainly be saved from such problems. In the rare situation where we might have to face some problems, we will be able to handle them much better.

Moreover, if we are in the good and capable hands of a true yogi, and are doing meditation under his direct guidance, we don't have to worry about such problems. But we must be really very fortunate to find such a yogi.

All great players have to go through several bad patches throughout their sports career. During such times, nothing seems to work for them. Those bad patches are like black nights of the soul for them. But, because of their single-minded, uni-directional efforts, great determination, winning spirit and, above all, their sportsmanlike spirit, they succeed in coming through those trying moments. Passing through such bad times is like a test for him to prove his talent and his calibre as a world-class player. It is true that those who survive bad times become stronger, whereas those who succumb to pressures perish.

The same kind of approach is needed for our fruitful survival in meditation. If we are playful, bad patches will come and go, but they will not disturb or distract us. They will not deter us from being on the path of meditation. We will continue to do well, in spite of those bad patches.

Except for a few subtle differences, being playful in meditation is similar to being playful in other games – and people should try and understand these subtle differences to be able to enjoy the game of meditation more.

First of all, there is always a goal to be reached while playing other games – you are supposed to play to win. In contrast, meditation is very different: we have to play this game to get ready to play the much larger 'divine game'. Meditation is a tool that helps us get equipped to participate and enjoy the natural glory of the divine play.

Unlike other games, the rules of the divine game are not framed by any human being. They are framed by the higher intelligence. Nobody has the authority to make any changes to these rules, and it is not possible, even if one wants to. If we understand these rules and stay within their ambit, we can use them to do well in meditation.

Similarly, to do well in the divine game, we have to learn to willingly accept and respect those rules.

We Should Be Without Any Expectations

If somebody asks us, 'Why do you meditate? What do you want to achieve through meditation? What is the purpose?' the only real answer is that we meditate for the joy of meditation and nothing else. The purpose of meditation is not different from meditation – it is an integral part of the actual process of meditation.

Those who practise meditation should always remember one thing. Just because we desire certain things does not mean that our desires will be fulfilled. And just because we do not desire anything, does not mean that we will not get anything.

We can see this dictum at work in the case of Jimmy Carter, who was actively involved in building homes for the homeless. He had a very good response from all over the USA for this truly philanthropic work. I recently met someone who is an active volunteer in this project. She told me how wonderful she feels after providing homes to the homeless. She also told me that Mr Carter, a former president of the United States, gets actively involved in the actual construction work as a physical labourer. He did this work without any expectations. But if the overwhelming response for this cause is any measure, it was far more than he could have asked for or expected.

There is a thriving spiritual-cum-social movement in India. It has been conceived, initiated and headed by a great man called Pandurangshastri Athavale. All members of this movement are popularly known as *swadhyayis* and their group as 'Swadhyay Parivar' ('Swadhyay' means self-study and 'parivar' means family). Swadhyay Parivar is a huge family of millions of *swadhyayis* from all over India and from other countries too. The *swadhyayis* go on a *bhakti pheri*, or a 'devotional round'. During this devotional round, they visit different houses, meet people and just remind them of the divine presence within them. Their only intention behind such home visits is to offer their tributes to the God who resides within the hearts of the people they visit.

The *swadhyayis* do not preach or give any religious sermons to the householders they visit; neither do they tell them what they should or should not do. They do not give any advice about giving up smoking or drinking alcoholic beverages or anything like that. They do not take up any position as social reformers. Yet this movement is spreading very fast and those who are participating in it are getting radically transformed into new human beings.

The devotees do not even expect or accept a cup of tea. Offering a cup of tea to a guest is in fact the least you can do, but *swadhyayis* do not even expect that from the host they visit. They just give their love to everybody, regardless of class, creed or religion.

The late Pandurangshastri Atavale started and nurtured this work, without asking for any help from anybody whatsoever, for the past several decades. By virtue of the sheer quality and magnitude of his philanthropic work, he was flooded with all kinds of help from all over the world.

We have to keep this dictum in mind while practising meditation. Just because we expect great things to happen during meditation, doesn't mean that they will actually happen. And just because we are practising meditation without any expectation does not mean that we will not get anything at all either. But we should not look at it as some kind of trick to be played for getting expected results. The results come only when we truly do not desire them.

In fact, if we are entirely focused on enjoying our meditation and are doing it wholeheartedly, the results will come as a natural consequence of what we are doing.

Devotion in Meditation

When we start practising meditation for the sheer joy of it, we automatically start doing it better, and the resultant improvement in meditation brings us closer to ourselves.

Through meditation, a great panorama of divine play is revealed to us. We start enjoying life more than ever before, because of our active participation in the wonderful play of the divine. Meditation gradually matures and reaches fruition when we start doing it in a joyful manner.

If we want to reach our spiritual destination much faster, we should never be worried about getting there, but just remain focused on doing it right. The harder we try to get there, the farther it moves away from us.

I am reminded of a beautiful story about Namdeo, which will clarify the point still further. Namdeo was a great saint and a true devotee. He belonged to the state of Maharashtra, where I come from. In Maharashtra, there is a famous temple of the God Vitthal. Hundreds of thousands of people from all over India visit this temple every year to offer their prayers to the Lord. The idol in this temple has his hands resting on both sides of his waist, unlike the usual idols of gods, which hold their hands open and in a blessing position.

Namdeo was a special devotee of the Lord Vitthal. He was a highly evolved person who always remained immersed in divine bliss. One day, he went to the God and said, 'Lord, I have a serious complaint against you.' Only a true devotee like Namdeo could dare to complain to the God himself. It is the beauty of the relationship between the God and his devotees.

Lord Vitthal was not in the least upset with his devotee for having a serious complaint against him. He assured Namdeo of complete pardon and told him not to have any fear or hesitation to report it to him. Namdeo continued, 'Oh Lord, it is quite unbecoming on your part to keep your hands resting on your waist all the time. Particularly when people come to offer prayers to you and lay themselves prostrate at your feet, you should take cognizance of their devotion and lift your hand from the waist to shower them with your blessings. Why don't you do that?'

The Lord Vitthal replied, 'My dear son, you are only looking at the apparent inappropriateness of my behaviour towards my devotees. But do you know that out of the thousands of so-called devotees who come to the temple, hardly anybody comes for the joy of meeting me. Everybody comes here with some selfish motives.'

The Lord continued, 'They may appear to be laying themselves prostrate before me and may also appear to offer me the choicest of flowers, but as you know, I am not easily moved by such superficial gestures. I am far more receptive to genuine love than anything else. Most of them come with an intention of asking something or other in return to their devotion towards me. You are among those handful of devotees, who come to me with a genuine love and affection for me, who do not ask for anything from me.

'And, you know from your personal experience, how much I care for a true devotee like you, how friendly and loving I can be with such devotees. I talk with you, eat whatever food you offer to me with joy. I also help Janabai (a well-known lady saint and a devotee of the Lord Vitthal) in her household work and wash dishes at Eknath's house.' (Eknath is the name of another great saint and devotee of the Lord Vitthal.)

I do not really know whether there was such a conversation or not and whether this story is true or not. I am not concerned about that – a story like this carries a very powerful message with it. To me, the message of the story is more important than the story itself. The message is – if you worship God with pure love and do not expect anything in return from Him, He becomes yours forever and showers you with all his blessings.

In the same way, if we study and practise meditation just for the pure joy of it, we will surely experience immense peace, bliss and blessings of being one with God. By being one with God, I do not mean being one with some idol sitting in the temple, but being an integrated, whole human being through regular practice of meditation and being one with the wholeness of the entire universe.

Idol worship is very useful for experiencing the wholeness within us becoming connected with the universal wholeness. Oneness with the whole of existence is a unique experience. If we remain on the right track of meditation from the very beginning, we will experience such wholeness much quicker than we expect it.

SECRET NUMBER FOUR

Develop A Genuine Taste
For Meditation

1

How to Develop a Taste for Meditation to Improve Mental Concentration

Even regular practitioners of meditation complain that they cannot focus their minds properly during meditation. It is because unknowingly they become too mechanical in the way they practise it: they don't find it interesting or they don't get any joy doing it. Inevitably, it becomes too boring to do it on a regular basis. Gradually, the motivation withers and they don't make much progress.

Experience is More Important Than Mere Information

The real issue here is not so much about learning how to focus our mind during meditation, but learning how to develop a true liking for meditation. Developing a true taste for something is a matter of experience. The first step in developing taste for something is to have a little exposure to its taste. We have to use this method with a child who is too fastidious about its eating habits. We have to cajole and coax the child to try different foods. If we as adults want to develop a taste for different foods, we have to first try them in small amounts.

There is a difference between talking about the sweetness of sugar and actually tasting it. We may know everything about the manufacturing of sugar: how the sugar cane is crushed, how to build a factory to crush it, from where the machinery is to be obtained, what different varieties of sugar are available in the market, etc. But unless we actually taste it, all this information would be meaningless. If we just take a small pinch of sugar and put it in our mouth, we can get a direct, immediate and first-hand experience of its sweetness. The importance and real worth of any knowledge can only be assessed in the context of actual experience.

Similarly, we may collect all sorts of information about meditation: the different techniques available, how they are supposed to be practiced, where to get the training, and so on. But all this information is meaningless if it is not followed by doing something concrete to get the direct, first-hand experience of meditation.

If we are seriously interested in learning meditation, we should not waste our precious time in merely collecting all such information, but pay more attention to the actual doing of meditation. The information is relevant only when we actually start learning meditation. Otherwise, it amounts to carrying an unnecessary burden in our head, which has no real worth of its own. Why carry such a load and waste our time and energy? It is like burdening our precious brain cells with worthless garbage and waste material.

Once we have the actual experience of meditation, there is hardly any need to collect more information than what is necessary to make progress in meditation. After we have made sufficient progress in the experiential knowledge of meditation, collecting further data about various techniques of meditation would probably have little significance. After the direct experience, nothing else really matters.

It is quite interesting to know that after mastering meditation, even if somebody is critical about it, we don't get upset about such comments. We don't feel the need to either justify or vehemently oppose the person. As long as we know the truth, what other people think about it hardly matters to us.

Actual Doing is Very Important

A famous author receives an invitation from a group of aspiring young writers to conduct a one-day seminar on 'How to be a successful writer'. On the day he asks the audience a simple question: 'How many of you are really interested in becoming a writer?'

Almost all the students raise their hands. The author tells them, 'If you are really serious about being a successful writer, my only advice to you is to go to your rooms and start writing.' After giving this advice, he declares that the seminar is over and leaves the hall. Surprisingly, the students rated this seminar as the best seminar of the year.

I think the author was absolutely right. If we want to learn something, we have to plunge ourselves into action. We will learn more about what we are doing through our actions than mere words, theories and descriptions.

This is true with meditation. In the beginning we do need some initial information about how to start. As we proceed on the path, we certainly have to get proper help and advice from time to time, according to the stage of spiritual evolution we have reached. However, all the while, the practical application of the knowledge should be emphasized rather than mere information. Actual 'walking' is far more important than anything else: those who 'walk' reach the destination and those who just 'talk' reach nowhere near their goal and get lost.

Once we actually taste the flavour of what it feels like to be in a state of meditation, we may choose to gather some information about other techniques of meditation that are described in the authentic scriptures on yoga. But now the situation is different. Having practised meditation for some time and experienced its actual flavour, it is quite fascinating to read the scriptures on yoga. At this point it is more like fun than collecting information. It has a very different meaning and significance. The most important point is that now we can read between the lines, where the real storehouse of wisdom from such literature lies.

It is an immense joy to tap the precious reservoir of wisdom contained in the scriptures. With the help of such wisdom, we can scan the facts we have gathered on meditation from other sources. The scanning is useful for making a right choice about the meditation which is most appropriate for our spiritual progress. When we choose an appropriate type of meditation, we make rapid advancement in meditation and concurrently develop a greater taste for it.

What is Spiritual Health and Wellbeing?

A patient once complained to me, 'Doctor, I had a problem in my stomach for which I went to a gastroenterologist. He advised me to undergo a long list of different tests and investigations. When he studied the reports of those tests, he could not find anything wrong with my body. I think I made a terrible mistake by going through the ordeal of those tests. I spent a lot of money, which was nothing but a colossal waste.'

The doctor had no choice in the matter: he had to conduct the investigations to arrive at a specific diagnosis to start a specific line of treatment, based on the findings of those tests.

I had to explain to the patient that the purpose of the investigations was to correctly diagnose the underlying pathology of the disease process and to confirm whether he was healthy or sick. I told him, 'Now, after the investigations, at least you know for sure that there is nothing wrong with your health. There is no organic pathology in your body to substantiate clinical findings. The doctor had no way of knowing this, without having the test reports in front of him. This information was necessary for him to decide about the exact line of treatment to be given to you. And that was the reason why he had to ask you to get those tests done.'

I took the opportunity to impress upon him the importance of starting yoga in earnest by saying, 'Now you know that you are healthy, so you can safely start with the full course of yoga. There are no restrictions on you.'

It is true that some medical investigations appear superfluous to patients. However, doctors recommend such procedures for several reasons. The foremost among them is of course to work towards a correct diagnosis and treatment. But they should be used more judiciously as patients are often wary of the medical fraternity and the high-tech procedures.

Something similar happens in the case of meditation. There are several methods of meditation to choose from. To find out which one among them is most suitable for us, it is very important that we start with the simple ones first. If they don't work after initial trials, it is better to approach the 'doctor of meditation' for consultation and advice. He is the right person who can 'diagnose' our problem and immediately 'prescribe' some 'remedy'. If he is not satisfied with the diagnosis, he may suggest we go through some 'spiritual investigations' to arrive at a proper diagnosis of our problem with meditation. The spiritual investigation is mostly in the form of a simple modification or slight refinement in our meditation practice. Thus, he gets a vivid picture of our problem. He may also decide to 'admit' us into his *ashram* or 'spiritual hospital' under his direct supervision and scrutiny while carrying out more 'sophisticated and advanced' spiritual investigations. In the light of his diagnosis, he prescribes a specific spiritual treatment. It is in the form of doing some spiritual experiments on us. We have to work on ourselves according to the 'spiritual treatment' he has prescribed to us for some time before we can expect any results. The best results come when we know which is the right meditation for our spiritual health. We have to spend some time, money and energy to get to the proper 'diagnosis' about which particular technique of meditation would be most appropriate for our 'spiritual health' and well-being. Obviously, it can't be considered as a wasteful effort.

Once our problems in meditation are correctly diagnosed and properly treated by a competent 'doctor of meditation', we begin to enjoy real spiritual health in the form of profound peace of mind and boundless inner joy. As this happens, our taste for meditation grows in leaps and bounds.

Appreciate, Don't Criticize

It is very important at this point to be careful not to talk in superlative terms about our own method of meditation and underrate others. What we like about our method is a matter of our individual taste and what others like about their meditation is theirs. To denigrate a different method is a sure sign of vanity. What we need to do is to verify the authenticity of our own progress in meditation, to see whether it is real or imaginary.

No meditation is either superior or inferior to any other meditation in absolute terms. What suits us best may not suit another person at all and vice versa. We have to do whatever is best suited to us and let others make their own choice. We need to learn to respect other techniques, too. There is no point in criticizing other methods of meditation, because such criticism does more harm to us than the method or the person whom we criticize. Why waste our precious time and energy in letting our mind get more agitated and restless?

It is interesting that a true meditator can identify and appreciate another meditator, even though he may be following an entirely different method of meditation. This happens just like a true artist really understands and appreciates the artwork of another artist.

Meditation is the most precious of the arts. It helps us realize the true meaning of the art of living. The art of meditation is practised on the inner canvas of individual awareness, which gradually merges with the universal awareness. Only a person who is grown in awareness through meditation can really see and appreciate what is drawn on the canvases of individual and universal awareness. Thus, they know the real meaning of being happy with oneself and being happy within oneself. Only a truly happy person develops a true taste for meditation.

2

Differentiate between a Taste for Meditation and a Taste for Other Things

Now we know that we can improve our mental concentration by developing a true taste for meditation. But the important question is whether there is any difference between the taste for meditation and other tastes? If so, what is it? Developing a true taste for meditation appears very difficult. What can we do to make it easier? How do we develop a liking for meditation?

What is the Underlying Motivation – Satisfaction or Dissatisfaction?

We 'like' certain objects, certain people and certain things from our surroundings and get attracted to them because of our liking for them. Obviously we do not like all the objects around us. We like some and dislike others. Our liking is 'exclusive' in nature and remains confined to certain objects only. When we like something, it is because of our individual choice.

For instance, when you are tired of eating the same chicken sandwich or cheese sandwich at home every day, you might feel like going out to dinner to eat a steak or enjoy a five-course French meal. If you like spicy food, you may go to an Indian restaurant. Over a period of time, we develop liking for different types and tastes of food.

A person who is truly mature, wise and has developed the right attitude towards life will not go out to eat steak just because he dislikes a chicken sandwich or a cheese sandwich prepared at home. He eats different food because he likes it as much as he likes his 'normal' food. So, he moves from one object of joy to another with ease and enthusiasm. He never complains, but enjoys whatever he is doing at a given moment. Naturally, he remains satisfied all the time and shares it with others too.

In the same way, there is a different kind of fun in being at home doing nothing or doing some household work at leisure or simply relaxing under a clear sky in the backyard. The joy of going out to attend an opera show is also a different kind of joy.

At a superficial level, it may appear that there is no difference between a person who is doing one thing because he has made a choice to do it and the other one who has not made such a choice. But deep down, their mental states could be quite different from each other. One who is planning to attend an opera because he is bored at home is going to spread his boredom further. If we are dissatisfied with something and that happens to be our motivation to do something else, we can never be truly happy in our life.

Being bored at times is quite natural. It only indicates that we are dissatisfied with something. If we try to run away from boredom, it grows. If we are 'friendly' towards our boredom, it quickly disappears. We have to try this to believe it.

It is therefore very important not to practice meditation because we want to avoid our day-to-day problems and run away from them. We should also not look at meditation as another novel pleasure that is different from other worldly pleasures.

Right from the beginning of our journey, we have to bear in mind that we have to practice meditation with a fulfilled mind. Our only motivation should be to personally explore, discover and experience the higher states of consciousness. If we practice meditation for the sheer joy of practice, it will reach fruition faster. It is a sure and powerful way of reaching higher states of consciousness, peace of mind and inner joy.

3

Differentiate between Inner Joy and Outer Joy

Developing a true taste for meditation is a matter of understanding the subtle differences between inner joy and outer joy. It also depends on the way we think and approach our life in general.

The Outer World is an Expression of the Inner World

Meditation is essentially a special type of inward journey, but it is never in conflict with any other journey in the outer world. The terms 'outer' and 'inner' are not mutually exclusive in nature. They are intimately connected and interwoven with each other and represent a fundamental reality of life. We cannot draw a line of demarcation between them. These terms are used for the sake of convenience of description and communication.

It is said that 'beauty lies in the eyes of the beholder'. An object appears beautiful to us not because it is actually beautiful, but because we are in a favourable inner state of being at the time we perceive that object. When such inner state gets in contact with the external object, it appears beautiful to us. The beauty also depends on our preconceived notions about it and the way we are trained to perceive and appreciate it.

The way we look at the external world gets modified according to our inner state. The world appears to us through the way we look at it. Whenever we look at an object, its image gets reflected in our consciousness. This image is evaluated according to our individual methods of evaluation. The same object may create different inner states, depending on individuals' methods of evaluation. The inner state transforms the way we look at the object. Therefore, the way an object appears to us depends on the way we look at it. That is why the world looks so different to different individuals.

An ordinary person would feel repulsed at the sight of a poor, shabby beggar in the street, but a compassionate person like Mother Teresa would take him home to bathe, clothe and feed him.

Looking at a beautiful dress on sale in an expensive shop creates different mental states in a man and his wife. The husband may feel like buying it for his wife, but looking at the price tag on the dress, she may feel like spending that money on her husband and children.

There is a beautiful saying in Sanskrit: 'The sins are not committed by our body, but by our mind.' When we greet a dear friend, a beloved spouse or a daughter with a hug and a kiss, our body remains the same in each case, but our feelings and inner states are quite different each time. The physical act of hugging and kissing remains the same, but the inner state of being is different each time.

As a meditator, we should understand the subtle differences between experiences of the outer world and the inner world. In this way, we can learn to manage them according to their real worth and individual merit. Thus, we can strike a wonderful balance between our worldly life and spiritual life.

Fundamental Approach Towards Life

Human beings are different from each other because they approach life differently. For instance, those who 'live to eat' are vastly different from those who 'eat to live'. Those who live to eat good food get attached to it and remain mentally engrossed in its taste. They are constantly preoccupied with thoughts about the food they have eaten or they are about to eat. Naturally, there is hardly any room left in their consciousness for other important issues like meditation. In contrast, those who eat to live never let thoughts about food or its taste occupy their mind for a long time. Both categories of people can eat the same food but, because they have different mind-sets, it tastes differently to them.

A person who is interested only in the food and its taste, eats it *for* the taste. Whenever he eats food, he wants to satisfy his palate with the taste. Such a person cannot really enjoy the food he is eating, because his mind remains preoccupied with expectations about the taste.

On the other hand, a person who is not very concerned about the taste of the food he is eating remains mentally free to enjoy its taste and appreciates it more. He eats it for the joy of eating. Other things do not matter to him. He enjoys whatever food he eats, regardless of its taste and therefore enjoys it more.

There is a world of difference between the attitude of a person who has sacrificed something *for* the sake of love and one who has sacrificed something *with* love. The one who has sacrificed for the sake of love tends to exploit it later to satisfy selfish personal interests. He keeps beating his own drum to cash in on the sacrifice. On the other hand, those who sacrifice something with love do it wholeheartedly. They do it so happily that they get a natural reward of inner satisfaction, without really striving for it. The results of their actions are built into the very act of their sacrifice.

The same thing happens in the case of a person who eats *for* the sake of joy and the one who eats *with* joy. One who eats with joy enjoys his food more, because he is not attached to its taste. On the other hand, one who eats food for the joy he derives from eating remains mentally attached to the food while he is eating it, as well as after it has been eaten.

If our mind is attached to food it will get constantly drawn towards its taste, flavour and so on. Naturally, we will not be able to practise meditation properly.

Grooming is Essential

Grooming our mind for the inward journey of meditation can be a little difficult. If our mind is lost in thoughts about different objects from the external world, this journey becomes more difficult than it should be. The practice of meditation will be very difficult for us if we are not able to keep our mind together and gently direct it inwards. We will not be able to enjoy meditation if it is too difficult for us, and if we don't enjoy it, we will not be able to do it on a long-term basis. Unless we practice meditation persistently and patiently for a long duration of time, we will not be able to make much progress on the path of spiritual evolution.

A person who is 'eating to live' and is 'sacrificing with love' is a different kind of person. He can stabilize his mind more easily and much faster too. He certainly knows the importance and usefulness of different objects that are available to him in the external world, but he never lets himself get carried away by those objects.

He knows that food is essential for survival, but he is more focused on understanding other important issues in life. He does not attach excessive importance to the food he eats, nor does he reduce its importance. Naturally, his mind is never caught up in thoughts about food he has eaten yesterday or is eating today or will eat tomorrow.

I always wonder why people make such a big fuss if the food they are eating is not to their taste or they find hair in their soup or the spaghetti sauce is too thin or too thick. The wisest thing to do is to simply eat something else or to adjust the taste so that it agrees with our likes and dislikes. There is no point complaining and wasting time on such trivial matters.

4

Relationship Between External Joy and Joy of Meditation

External Pleasures

A person who is after material pleasures keeps thinking about those pleasures all the time. He keeps constantly complaining about trivial things too. He complains about not having enough pleasures. After he gets some pleasures, he grumbles that they are not adequate and up to his expectations. In short, he moans about *having* the pleasures as well as *not having* them. Such a person is dissatisfied 'with' pleasures and 'without' pleasures too.

When a person who is constantly running after pleasures turns to the practice of meditation, he/she seldom does so because he is interested in learning meditation. He/she wants to learn meditation because he is thoroughly tired of his/her routine pleasures.

For most people like that, meditation provides a welcome change in their routine. They are interested in pursuing a different kind of pleasure through meditation. Some of them do it because they 'want' peace of mind. Some do it because they want to proudly talk about it at parties with their friends.

In India, many people go on a religious fast either once a week or at least once a fortnight. You can choose any day of the week, because every day is an auspicious day for the devotees of one deity or the other. You have a wide choice too, because there are hundreds of deities available for worship. But on such days people don't really fast in the real sense. They only eat specially prepared food that is supposed to be eaten only on the fast days. This special food for the fast is so delicious that the devotees wind up eating more food on those days than they usually eat. Paradoxically, therefore, many of those who fast on one day suffer from indigestion or a bad stomach the next day.

Can we say that a religious fast is successful if it is followed by indigestion? No, we can't, because the very purpose of fasting is defeated if it leads to indigestion. Real fasting involves giving the digestive system a complete rest so as to restore and revitalize its digestive power. It has a definite physiological purpose and significance.

Meditation is Not for 'Change'

Traditionally in India, all healthy practices are in some way or another connected with religious rites. It is certainly a very smart way of inculcating healthy habits in the minds of the general populace. Religious fasting is one such practice. The great religious masters from the past thought that it would be more appropriate to ask people to do something as a religious as well as a physical activity. When you are doing religious fasting it is expected that, apart from not eating anything, you will spend all your time in prayer and philosophical reflection. But over the years, many things have completely changed. People doing religious fasts seem to have completely forgotten its true meaning and real significance.

Therefore, it will be wrong if we start practicing meditation with an intention of enjoying a different *kind* of pleasure than usual. By doing so, we will only fool ourselves, but will never know what real meditation is.

Bondage Of Worldly Pleasures

If we carefully observe and study the limitations of various mundane things that are happening around us, we can easily understand the inherent limitations of worldly pleasures. Worldly pleasures do not satisfy our desires completely. On the contrary, fulfilment of one desire breeds new set of desires that need fulfilment. And, the cycle keeps repeating all the time. The most important limitation of every desire is its short lived nature or 'transience'. Although every pleasure is transient, one's desire for pleasures is 'infinite'. Therefore, there is an on-going inner war between transience and infinity. After having understood this process, we can keep our desires within limits and then we will be able to practice meditation more effectively and enjoy it more too. Not only that, but we will also know how to enjoy worldly pleasures and still remain free of their bondage. By doing so, our mind will not linger in the outer world. Naturally, it will be available to go into the inner world. Once we know what it means to enter the inner world, the quality of our meditation practice will begin to improve substantially.

After we have started doing meditation properly, it takes quite some time before we develop a true taste for it. This is the most difficult part of the journey. We have to keep trying and be very patient.

Continuous practice of meditation without losing patience is possible only when we have the right mental attitude.

Being Free Of Attractions

We do not need to give up pleasures to be able to direct our attention inwards. What we need to do is to be free of the craving for such pleasures. And unless we do that, we will not be able to practice meditation properly or develop liking for it.

Being free of attractions also does not mean that we should never enjoy worldly pleasures or give them up superficially, or turn our back on them. What we have to do is to discover and realize the binding influence of such pleasures on our mind. Once we realize the suffering that goes with such bondage, we will be free of it. Once we are free of the suffering and bondage, we will be free of the attraction to such pleasures. When an excessive attraction for worldly pleasures is reduced to a minimum, our mind becomes free of the disturbing thoughts related to such pleasures and will therefore not get drawn towards them.

Meditation Happens

Thereafter, practising meditation will be very easy, because our mind will remain silent during meditation as well as at other times. Whenever our mind becomes silent during meditation, we come in direct contact with our true self, which is seated at the core of our being. A contact with the true self is an experience of bliss. As this contact grows stronger and stronger, proportionately our joy in meditation also grows. Once we start getting true joy through meditation, we start looking forward to doing it every day and our mind begins to get settled much faster. At that stage there is no need to try hard to concentrate during meditation. It starts happening on its own and without much effort. Once we have reached this stage, real progress on the path of meditation begins.

SECRET NUMBER FIVE

*Find Proper Help from a
True Master*

1

Don't Judge the Person by External Appearance

Inner State is More Important than the External Manifestation

For the mind to remain attentive during meditation, one needs to develop a true taste for it. We have to put in honest effort to develop such taste.

It is also necessary to take proper guidance from a genuine spiritual master. The person whom we want to approach for assistance should not be a mere academic person, who has learned about meditation by rote. He should be the one who has actually experienced the highest state of consciousness through meditation himself.

Only a truly experienced person can possibly help others. We have to be very careful when making a judgement about a person with spiritual experience and wisdom. One should never go by his external appearance, but explore deeper for signs of true knowledge and wisdom in him.

It is extremely important to discern what a person actually *is*, not just how he *looks*. While taking such guidance, one should pay more careful attention to the actual learning of meditation, and be careful not to get carried away by the external appearance of the teacher. It is also necessary to read between the lines while listening to his spoken words or reading the suggested literature. This helps us understand the deeper meaning and significance of the spoken and written words.

It is important to know that meditation is essentially an inner state and we have to find a technique of meditation that is most suitable for us to be able to reach an actual experience of such a state. After the initial choice is made, we have to focus our attention on mastering the technique. While doing so, we have to refrain from using external yardsticks to make an assessment about our progress in meditation. The wrong yardsticks often lead to wrong assessments. Wrong inferences drawn on such assessments invariably result in wrong decisions about a future course of action and consequently, causes serious problems in our spiritual progress.

Being Good is More Important than Just Appearing Good

While living in the mundane world, it is usually enough to follow certain norms of behaviour that are generally approved by society. If we are decent in character and in dealing with others, we can generally expect our worldly life to be comfortable and without too many problems.

But it is not the same when it comes to our inner world. Mere 'good behaviour' is not enough in this world. It should always be accompanied by a genuine inner goodness. Good behaviour should be a spontaneous outward expression of a corresponding 'goodness within'. Therefore, 'looking good' is not enough; 'being good' from within is also equally important.

What we feel is an internal process, whereas how we behave or appear to others is an outward manifestation of our inner feelings.

In our day-to-day life, as long as we do not cause any nuisance to others, people are fine with us. As long as we are dealing with them properly, they are not concerned about knowing our real feelings about them. They are not at all interested in knowing whether our good behaviour towards them is a result of real goodness within us or not.

As far as our inner world is concerned, how we appear to others is not important. What matters most is what we actually *are* inside. Being good is far more important than looking good. In a spiritual context, as long as we are good from within, it hardly matters whether we are equally good looking in our appearance or not. Ashtavakra was a great sage from ancient India. He had several physical disabilities, but was highly spiritually evolved. He wrote a classic treatise on yoga called *Ashtawakra*

Geeta. As far as his external looks were concerned, he was very ugly. But at a spiritual level, he was very beautiful. His spiritual understanding was of such a high order that the great king Janaka, a highly evolved yogi himself, requested him to be his guru or a spiritual guide in the higher aspects of spiritual *sadhana*. Janaka could do this only because he was not influenced by the external ugliness of Ashtavakra.

Use Your Insight to Identify a Truly Wise Person

While taking guidance on meditation from a liberated and wise person, we should not be too concerned about external measures of evaluation such as how he looks, how he dresses, how big his following is, or whether he has written any books or not. Wisdom lies in being more attentive to the deeper meaning and significance of his words, behaviour and teachings.

It requires a special skill and ability to see things in the same holistic manner as a realized master. His simple external appearance could be highly misleading. If he is the real treasure of wisdom then we should never miss the opportunity of learning the secrets of meditation from such a person and thus benefit from his teachings. We have to remember that a genuinely wise person is never after superficial or cheap publicity. It is therefore quite possible that we may not have heard about him at all. Naturally, we will have to make extra special effort to discover such a person. People do eventually recognize and acknowledge his simplicity, serenity and greatness.

If you come across a mystic like Shankar Maharaj, you will probably not find anything attractive or worth liking in his appearance. It is said that when Shankar Maharaj used to go into a state of deep trance, saliva used to literally pour out of his mouth. On many occasions, he used to abuse people who went to meet him. Sometimes, he used unsophisticated words and filthy language while talking to them. He used to smoke cigars too. But those who knew him well said that he was truly a wise and liberated person. One might feel puzzled as to how those people could have recognized his wisdom. But the answer is easy: they were the people who could completely overlook his external appearance and appreciate the spiritual authority that lay hidden under such appearance. Maharshi Vinod, my father, was very close to Shankar Maharaj. Maharshi did a special spiritual ritual to revive the cadaver of Shankar Maharaj, to receive the last message for his disciples.

Upasani Maharaj was yet another mystic who was also an authentic spiritual master. He used to live on a garbage dump and threw stones at people who came to see him. But he was a great authority on the Vedas, the most ancient spiritual literature known to mankind.

A true sage is not concerned about whether people accept their spiritual authority or not. For such people, it does not make any difference whether others are impressed by their wisdom or not. They are not worried about what impression other people have of them.

Ramakrishna Paramahansa was known as a 'mad priest' during his times. Anywhere, at any time, for any minor reason, he would go into a state of deep transcendental trance. Vivekananda was his favourite disciple, who did not pay much attention to the apparent madness of this priest, but tried to fathom this special kind of madness to discover the spiritual authority of this wonderful person, and made him his guru. History proves that he made the right decision, because it brought radical transformation in his life. This was possible because Vivekananda could connect with Ramakrishna in the realm of real self, which is the substratum of all existence.

At this point, we have to be clear about certain things. It is true that a filthy-looking person is not necessarily 'filthy' on the inside. He could in fact be a liberated person. But it is also not true that every dirty-looking person who abuses and beats people is a true master.

Similarly, a simple-looking person may not be all that simple inside. It is wrong to assume that someone who is immaculately dressed in expensive clothes is not likely to be a liberated person.

One thing is certain – our physical vision is not good enough to accurately evaluate whether a person is liberated or not. A fully developed inner vision is what we need for this purpose. It is more important what our inner vision tells us about a person than how he looks to our mortal eyes.

2

How to Develop Inner Vision

Learn How to Enter the Mind

We must understand how to develop our inner vision to find the right person from whom we should learn meditation. Without a doubt, it cannot be learned in a classroom. Nowadays, we know that there are classes for almost everything: 'how to love', 'how to win people over', 'how to get promoted in your job' and so on. Under the circumstances, one should not be surprised to find an advert for a class on 'developing an inner vision'.

The best way to develop our inner vision is to keep our eyes open to observe the things happening around us and to go through every experience with an unbiased mind. We mustn't judge anyone by their looks, but try to understand the deeper layers of their mind. We have to make a special effort to trust our inner feelings too.

In today's world, in most educational institutes and probably in the educational system as a whole, we see that more emphasis is placed on how one presents oneself to others than what one's real individual feelings and perceptions are. This is why we never learn to respect our genuine feelings. We presume that whatever we feel in our heart is likely to be wrong or false. When this happens regularly and over a long time, we start losing faith in our inner feelings. Lack of faith eventually gives rise to a tendency to look at everything one feels with suspicion. This is precisely what happens to most people.

The situation at home is no different from educational institutes. Parents seldom encourage their children to speak freely from their hearts about their true feelings. They keep giving instructions, suggestions, and orders to their wards. Children hardly get an opportunity to do things they like to or 'feel' like doing. Slowly, children learn to disregard their true feelings. They do not develop any need to discover their true feelings and be honest about them. Even if they feel such a need, they are so hard pressed for time that they cannot spare enough time to undertake this search. That is why they never develop an ability to know and appreciate what they really feel. They don't get taught how to develop their feeling faculty. Consequently, this capacity remains rudimentary. Naturally, their inner vision also remains stunted, because it is an ability to see and understand something with the help of our inner feelings.

As a result, one gets caught up in a pernicious habit. A habit of forming an opinion about another person, not on what one genuinely feels about him/her from within oneself, but on the way he dresses, whether he owns a car or not, whether he stays in a big house or an apartment, and whether he is in possession of all the worldly comforts or not.

Slowly, one begins to erroneously believe that such material pleasures and comforts are the real signs of success and greatness. One nurtures the wrong notion that having such comforts automatically makes the person great. How all those comforts were collected and where he got all the money for them become unimportant and irrelevant issues. Being affluent is what really matters most! It is alright even if there is no true happiness and contentment in life. With money one can always buy anything and everything.

Due to this wrong way of thinking and incorrect attitude towards life, one becomes too carnal or too materialistic in one's outlook. It is almost impossible for such a person to understand the subtlety of inner vision. Consequently, the qualities of knowledge and wisdom are replaced by outer signs of material affluence.

Being Free of the Influence of 'Body-bound'-ness

Around 50 to 60 years ago, learnedness was greatly respected in India. In those days, scholarship was held in higher esteem than material richness. The inner treasure of knowledge and wisdom was considered more important than the outward display of money and affluence. My father Maharshi Vinod was a well-known thinker, brilliant scholar, saint and a yogi. Admiring his inner spiritual wealth, my mother married him. She was herself a great Sanskrit scholar and a gold medallist in the state-level higher secondary school examination held in 1926. My father had diabetes when they got married, and he was the father of a nine-year-old mentally challenged boy with special educational needs from his previous marriage. It was his third marriage. His earlier two marriages ended in tragedy, as his wives died soon after he married them. A truly liberated person like him was not expected to marry three times. Still he married, because he had to keep the promise he had given to his parents that he would continue the family tradition and lineage. I am happy that he did marry for the third time, otherwise I wouldn't have been here to write this book!

My mother did not pay much attention to the fact that it was his third marriage and that he had a mentally challenged child from the previous marriage whom she would have to bring up. She respected his scholarship and wisdom. My father was very handsome, though my mother wasn't all that beautiful. My father did not look at her external beauty, but attached more importance to her erudition, competence and confidence.

I still remember one incident very vividly. One morning, my father was walking down the street. Lord Abasaheb Mujumdar, who belonged to a princely family, was coming towards him from the opposite side of the road. As soon as Mujumdar saw my father, he quickly got down from his horse-driven carriage and laid himself prostrate before my father, in the middle of a busy street. While doing so, the ego of his Lordship did not get in the way. That is why he could pay obeisance to the great wisdom and knowledge of my father. He was above the influence of his gross vision.

3

The Usefulness of Inner Vision

At this point, if inner vision is so important, one may wonder what is the role and significance of our normal physical vision in understanding the deeper significance of life? What is the meaning of external beauty in a meditator's life?

Differentiate between the Means and an End

We perceive physical reality with the help of our physical vision and to that extent our mortal vision is useful to us. It has its own significance too. It helps us connect with the outer world and lead our life well. Similarly, external beauty is essential and important in its own right. It makes the world colourful, attractive and interesting. However, we need to develop a special skill to perceive and appreciate inner beauty. Like external beauty, it is also quite real.

Inner vision is very useful for those who are interested in learning meditation. In the absence of such vision, it is not possible to explore the inner world properly. If our inner vision is underdeveloped, reaching the deeper layers of consciousness through meditation will be difficult.

It goes without saying that the means we use for realizing our goal must be in line with what we want to achieve. A knife used for cutting vegetables would not be used for cutting wood; a mixer used for mixing cement and sand for construction work cannot be used for mixing food; scissors used by a barber cannot be used for a surgical operation.

Once we are clear about what we want to achieve in life, we have to use proper tools to reach our goal. Inner vision is one such tool. Those who chase after carnal pleasures do not understand the intrinsic worth of this tool. Inner vision is useful for those who appreciate of that external beauty is only skin deep: they are strongly motivated to explore and discover what lies hidden behind such beauty. A well-developed inner vision is key in such explorations – it helps us delve deep within our being and that of others as well.

We Can Understand the Inner Nature

Inner vision is useful in recognizing the true master from whom one should learn the art of meditation. It is useful in several other areas too, but we have to observe great care and caution while putting it to such use. It develops well if we use it judiciously in a disciplined and subtle manner.

The overall quality, breadth, depth and expanse of self-awareness improves with inner vision. The way a person with expanded awareness thinks, acts and behaves is vastly different from other people. A person with a well-developed inner vision can perceive and understand many things which others cannot. It is not easy to decipher meaning from the words and actions of such a person.

A disciple goes to a town to collect alms for himself and his guru. He cooks food from the food grains he receives in the form of alms. With great reverence and love he offers this food to his guru. The guru, however, refuses to eat it. Confounded by the refusal, the disciple wonders whether there was anything wrong in his cooking. The question, 'Why did my revered guru decline from eating the food?' keeps bothering him. Ultimately, he decides to approach the guru for an explanation. The guru explains, 'I know that you have prepared this food with all your love in it. But I do not feel like eating it. I am getting very strong negative vibrations from the food. The person from whom you received the alms must have been a very bad person. Otherwise, there is no reason why I should not feel like eating this food. You may go to the town and find out what kind of person he is and let me know about it after you return.' The disciple rushes to the town to investigate and to his great surprise discovers that the person concerned was indeed a sinner: he had amassed wealth through unscrupulous means and had ruthlessly exploited the weak and helpless people to accumulate huge treasures of wealth. The guru had a highly developed inner vision. With the help of such vision he could easily sense the truth about this person and his moral background, which was the reason why he could not eat the food that was prepared from the alms received from this person's house.

Usefulness of Inner Vision in Everyday Life

A well-developed inner vision is quite useful in our day-to-day affairs too. Suppose a person comes to meet you with an attractive business proposal and offers a highly lucrative financial deal. If your well-developed inner vision indicates that there is something fishy or dubious about this person, it would be like a great asset to you. You would get an opportunity to exercise caution before you made a final decision about signing a deal with him. Taking heed of such a sign can go a long way and save you from heavy financial losses.

Possessing such special ability is truly a great asset in today's world. We are bombarded all the time by advertisements, trying to lure us into buying different things. If our decision to make a purchase is based on the superficial appearance and external feel of the product, we become vulnerable to buying unnecessary things. We can avoid this by making use of our inner vision. It will reveal to us what is good and bad in the product that we might plan to buy and thus help us make the right decision about buying. It will save us from getting carried away by the glittering exterior of the things on sale.

Benefits are By-products

Special classes to develop inner vision as a part of the consumer society are unlikely to stop such unethical practices. Inner vision cannot be developed just because it is useful in our day-to-day affairs. The benefits are more like by-products than anything else. It would be wrong on our part to take up meditation for the sole purpose of benefiting from it in this way. By doing so, even if we get those benefits, they will be temporary and superficial in nature. If we practise meditation just for the joy of it – without any expectation or the specific intention of 'What is in it for me?' – we will get more lasting benefits.

The famous Indian war – the Mahabharat, between the Kauravas and the Pandavas, as depicted in the well-known epic of *Mahabharata* – was about to begin. Lord Krishna placed an option for consideration before the great warrior Arjuna, from the side of the Pandavas, and Duryodhana from the opposite side. He asked them to choose between himself and his huge army for fighting the ensuing war. Arjuna quickly chose Lord Krishna and Duryodhana chose the army. Arjuna knew for sure that if the god was on his side, everything else would automatically fall into place and he would not have to worry about anything. He also knew that the whole army – cavalry, strategy and weapons – would be worthless if the God was not on his side.

What happened later proves beyond any trace of doubt that Arjuna was really wise in choosing Lord Krishna: he got wise counsel from the Lord at every critical moment throughout the war, which ultimately brought victory to the Pandavas. Lord Krishna guided Arjuna's chariot and gave proper advice to him from time to time.

Being someone of great perception, Duryodhana could only see how big the army was. He was very happy to have the army on his side, thinking that the size of the army was crucial in winning the war. However, he was disappointed in the end, because victory kept constantly eluding him. Duryodhana was obsessed with winning the war, but he could not foresee the decisive role played by Lord Krishna in the outcome of the war.

Arjuna was also very eager to win, but he was wise too. He chose the god because he loved him very dearly and also respected him. He knew the value of a close companionship with the god, who was going to guide his chariot throughout the war.

The moral of the story is that Arjuna was a worldly and spiritually wise person. He chose Lord Krishna because he loved and respected him. Winning the war came as a by-product of his companionship with the Lord. Duryodhana was only a worldly wise person. He therefore chose the army, but lost the war.

I had a very interesting experience a few years ago. A political leader of great stature used to come to me to learn Yoga. He was very happy with my teaching and, without my asking for anything from him, offered: 'Doctor, if you have any personal matter pending with the Government, please let me know. I will get it done immediately.'

I politely refused the offer and said, 'Thank you very much for your kind gesture, but I am happy with whatever I have at the personal level. I am very happy to be of some help to you through yoga. I do not want to take any personal favours from you, mainly because you cannot give me what I really seek and I am not interested in what you want to offer. Moreover, if I really want something, I will prefer to directly ask for it from God as I strongly believe that He is the real provider of everything.'

I didn't really want to be mean or rude to him by not accepting his help. I knew that he had offered it with love, affection and respect. But I was looking at him as my dear student of yoga and did not want him to upset our student–teacher relationship. He was taken by surprise by my 'strange' behaviour! He usually met people who always wanted something or other from him, because he was a well-connected politician. He hardly ever met anybody like me who was not even willing to accept what he had happily offered.

Do Not Deceive Yourself

It is true that everything is possible in this world, once our inner vision is fully developed. However, we have to refrain from getting caught in self-deception under the name of inner vision. It may lead to making false claims like, 'I am right, because it is my inner call', 'I do not need to give any explanation for my actions, because I have a well-developed inner vision'. Such claims are very dangerous, particularly when they are false. One may fall prey to wrong notions and start exploiting people on the strength of such flimsy assertions. It may trigger a chain reaction of false claims, posing a serious threat to our spiritual as well as material progress.

4

Understand the Limitations of Outward Expression

It is extremely difficult to discern the subtle differences in motivation behind any manifest behaviour. An ordinary person and a spiritually wise person may appear very similar in terms of their outward behaviour, but their inner state of being and the reasons behind their behaviour are likely to be poles apart. If one fails to comprehend this difference, one may make mistakes when assessing visible behaviour; if one understands the nature of manifest reality, such mistakes can be easily avoided.

The Motive Behind an Action is More Important

Suppose a spiritually wise person and an ordinary person are seen to be relishing the same kind of food. Their actions while eating are going to be very similar at a superficial level, but the underlying motives could be vastly different. Motives are a part of the interior milieu and are not readily visible to others. Due to an ingrained human tendency to assume that only what is visible is real, one tends to forget that reality is far more than what is visible to our eyes.

What is visible to us is just like the tip of an iceberg. What is hidden beneath is far greater than what is visible to us on the surface. Therefore, one who assumes that only what is visible is real is mistaken.

When a young man offers a beautiful rose to his sweetheart, it is an outward expression of his feelings of love and tenderness towards her. This visible gesture is only an infinitesimal part of the boundless love he harbours in his heart.

Similarly, while watching the extraordinary beauty of nature, an unseen creative urge can be triggered in some people. This may find expression in the form of a poem or a painting. But the real creative urge that is hidden within us is much greater than what its outward expression can represent. For most people, reality is limited to whatever is visibly apparent. We believe only what we can see. A boy and a girl who are in love always expect a vivid expression of such love from each other. The expression could be anything from a gesture to an articulated expression of love to an offering of a nice gift. It is like a physical commitment, which gives a sense of security and reassurance.

The Cause of Manifest Lies in the Unmanifest

In contrast to that of most people, the perception of a spiritually wise person is entirely different. He is fully aware of the fact that the invisible or 'unmanifest' reality is much bigger than the manifest one.

I would like to narrate a very apt story that relates to this. It is from the *Chhandogya Upanishad,* one of the most ancient spiritual texts. A guru asks his disciple to get a fruit from a tree. He then asks him, 'Do you know what this is?' The disciple replies, 'It is a fruit.' 'Cut this fruit and tell me what is there inside it,' orders the guru. The disciple cuts open the fruit and says, 'There is a pulp of the fruit.' After eating the pulp with the disciple, the guru asks him to break open one of the seeds and further asks, 'What is there inside the seed?' The disciple replies, 'Sir, There is "nothing" inside. I can only see an empty space.' The guru explains to him, 'It means that the "cause" of the visible fruit lies inside this empty space. Without a seed, there can't be any tree and without a tree there can't be any fruit. It means that the seed is the cause of the tree. As the cause of the fruit lies hidden in the seed, the cause of seed must also be present inside the seed. But, as you break open the seed, you do not find anything there. In conclusion, we may say that the presence of "invisible" space inside the seed is responsible for the "visible" existence of a seed and the visible seed for the tree and its fruits.'

Interdependence of Manifest and Unmanifest

From this story, we may also conclude not only that what is visible to our mortal eye is real, but what is invisible to it is also equally real.

One may raise a pertinent question here. 'Can nothingness be a cause of something that actually exists?' The answer to this question is 'yes' as well as 'no'. Our mortal eye cannot see what is inside the seed. In this sense, 'nothingness' inside a seed is the cause of the 'visible' seed. But just because our mortal eye cannot see something does not mean that really there is nothing inside. We can't see it because we lack the capacity to see it with our mortal eyes. In this sense, that 'something' inside the seed is the cause of the 'actual' seed.

After thoroughly washing our hands with soap and water, we may think that they are clean, but if we take a closer look under a powerful microscope, we may find many micro-organisms present. Our physical eyes cannot perceive what our amplified vision can see with the help of a microscope. Amplified vision does not create anything new, but we can see what is actually present there.

Now theories in physics also conclude that if we go on dividing atoms, we finally reach subatomic particles that are tinier than the atoms. Inside those particles, there is only an empty space.

This nothingness or empty space within is known as unmanifest reality, or *Avyakta Brahma,* and what is visible to our eyes is known as manifest reality, or *Vyakta Brahma.* The manifest comes into existence from the unmanifest. The manifest, in the course of time, fades away to become merged with the unmanifest. In other words *Avyakta Brahma* is the cause of *Vyakta Brahma* and *Vyakta Brahma* the cause of *Avyakta Brahma.* One cannot exist without the other.

5

Unseen and Seen are Both Equally True

Limitations of Visible Reality

Most people believe that reality consists only of what is visible to them, and therefore the realm of their experiences remains limited. They only see part of the reality, but believe it to be complete. As they see and accept only an incomplete reality, they believe in things that are manifest, visible and within the domain of their sense organs. Naturally, they enjoy only those pleasures that are perceptible to those sense organs and get completely caught up in them.

A wise *sadhaka*, who is a regular practitioner of meditation, relishes apparent reality with the sense organs as others do, but he *also explores and discovers the invisible dimensions of visible reality.* Thus, he understands the complete reality. Because he is able to grasp the known as well as unknown aspects of reality, his perceptions become more complete and more enriched in nature. Not only does he know 'invisible emptiness' as the real cause of the visible world, but also dares to completely trust this experience. He enjoys manifest reality, but doesn't get too embroiled in it. He develops a unique courage and strength to trust the invisible. This outstanding ability becomes the hallmark of such a person.

Judge the Invisible from What is Visible

It is comparatively easy to believe in what is apparent – it is right in front of us and is readily visible. However, it requires a great deal of courage to understand and believe what is hidden in darkness.

When Lata Mangeshkar, an internationally famous singer from India, was very young, her guru could see a tremendous hidden talent in her, which nobody else could see. He put trust in her talent and also taught young Lata to believe in her genius. He gave proper and timely guidance and groomed her into the successful singer that she became, recipient of the 'Bharatratna' (Jewel of India), the highest Indian civilian honour. Now, everybody offers praise and showers accolades on her. She has appeared in the *Guinness Book of World Records*. Now it hardly requires any expertise to appreciate and praise her genius. But it was surely very difficult to foresee her great future when she was a 'nobody'.

Similarly, Mr Acharekar, the famous cricket coach from India, identified child prodigy Sachin Tendulkar when he was nobody in cricket. Acharekar gave proper training, encouragement and guidance to Sachin in such a beautiful manner that he blossomed into a great batsman, and also was the recipient of the 'Bharatratna'. The late cricket legend Sir Don Bradman saw many similarities between his batting and that of Sachin.

By looking at the early expression of talent and potential in Lata and Sachin, their respective gurus dared to put faith in the 'invisible' potential of their disciples. They also taught them to have faith in themselves. It is surely a demonstration of an extraordinary courage by the gurus and their disciples. Both disciples have now achieved what is considered unparalleled success in their respective fields.

It is not easy to judge the vast hidden potential in someone by merely looking at a small expression of such potential, especially when it is at a nascent stage. The late Jiddu Krishnamurti is widely regarded as a genuine spiritual master of the twentieth century. He not only taught his philosophy of life to thousands, but also lived it himself. When he was barely nine or ten years old, Annie Besant and Leadbeater, two well-known Theosophists, could clearly see the future world teacher in him. Jiddu, the young Krishnamurti, was playing on the seashore when Leadbeater first saw him. He found that Jiddu's aura was very special, because it was as clear as a crystal. Auras are etheric fields around the person: their expanse, colour, clarity and glow reflect the person's inner state. Leadbeater was thoroughly astounded and dazzled by the extraordinary aura of Jiddu. Leadbeater and Besant adopted Jiddu and brought him up with great love and care to bring out the dormant world teacher in him.

6

How Does One Become an Authority?

Not all of us are fortunate to receive authentic guidance from a spiritual master like Krishnamurti. But one thing is certain: we do need such guidance for proper understanding of the practice of meditation. Guidance is also essential in order to make progress in meditation. The real problem is how to know whether a particular person is a true master or not. How do we make a right decision in this regard? Is there any way of certifying the authority of a spiritual master? What is one supposed to do to become a true master?

Authority in Day to Day Life

We can determine whether a particular medical practitioner is an authority in medicine or not by looking at his qualifications. Whether he is a good doctor or not can also be judged by knowing how many patients come to his clinic and how many of them get well after his treatment. The expertise of a building contractor can be ascertained by visiting various buildings and complexes constructed by him. The culinary skills of a chef can be confirmed by tasting the food he cooks.

Authority in meditation and spirituality can be judged by observing the behaviour of a person who claims to be a spiritual master and by the way he conducts himself. If he is genuine, you will find that his whole persona is filled with serenity, joy, cheerfulness, love and total self-awareness. He always looks like a truly integrated person. As he is constantly in a state of meditation, its deep influence is clearly evident in his day-to-day living.

Developing Authority In Meditation

It is obvious that those who are only interested in spending 10-15 minutes on meditation in the morning and 10-15 minutes in the evening are not likely to develop such authority. Similarly, it is unlikely that a person whose only intention behind practising meditation is to treat his health problem or to make his mind a little calmer could ever become an authority in meditation.

Spiritual masters are people who are deeply involved in meditation and related subjects. The main mission and goal of their life is meditation and they are totally committed to this goal. Naturally, because of their involvement and sincerity, they gradually develop a great deal of expertise in the subject to teach meditation to others. It is true that there can be no expertise without devoted and consistent practice, and without expertise one cannot be an authority in any field.

Expertise Comes Through Practice

If one wants to become an expert or an authority in any field, the first thing to be done is to find out what one's true affinity is. Once that is done, one should focus one's attention on finding out where to get an opportunity to pursue the aptitude and make a career out of it. After that, one should spend all the time available in a thorough study of the chosen field. It should be done with utmost sincerity, dedication and total involvement to understand the general as well as subtle dimensions of the field.

The main purpose behind such study should never be only to establish our authority over other people. It should be done for the sheer joy of learning, for true love for the subject. An in-depth study like this should be a high quality piece of work. Such work would automatically bring expertise to the person and expertise would endow natural authority to him/her.

In contrast, if one studies an important subject like meditation just for the sake of commanding authority over others, the quality of the meditation practice will suffer a great deal. And low-quality practice can never bring expertise or authority.

It is Only for Love, Not for Authority

I know one housewife who is a great cook. She cooks for the joy of cooking and not for winning accolades. She likes to see the faces of her family and friends lit with joy and satisfaction when they eat a hearty meal that she has so lovingly prepared. She puts all her heart and soul into her cooking. She doesn't mind the hard work involved in cooking because she loves and cares for the people she is cooking for. Serving the family well is a matter of joy and great satisfaction to her. Naturally, she is also cared for, respected and loved by her family; family members seek her advice in important matters – her authority has come through love and sacrifice.

It is equally true in meditation. Those who meditate with joy and share it with others, with pure unconditional love, will enjoy authority without striving for it. But those who try to manoeuvre themselves into a position of authority will never get it.

Let us therefore seek pure love, not authority. Authority will follow.

7

The Qualities of a True Master

They Don't Throw their Weight Around

It is a pleasure to watch a person who is a real authority but does not throw his weight around in society. A person who is really in control does not need to make any conscious, purposeful efforts to show his prowess. He is so sure of himself and his abilities that he needs no external props to substantiate his strength. His self-confidence is of a very high order. He knows with great certainty that if time demands it, he can demonstrate his extraordinary talent, which will be automatically visible to other people around him.

In this context, there is a beautiful story of Birbal. Birbal was well known for his intelligence, presence of mind, wisdom, common sense and witticism. He was the jewel of the court of King Akbar. The neighbouring king once decided to test the mettle of Birbal. He invited him to his court. Birbal did not understand why he had been invited, but decided to go anyway. Birbal was received in the kingdom with great dignity and honour. When he got down from his chariot to enter the court, he saw six people, dressed exactly like the king, sitting on six thrones. He immediately knew the real motive behind the invitation. He carefully studied all the so-called 'kings', then went straight to the real king, to pay his respect. The king was utterly surprised and asked Birbal how he had instantly recognized the real king from the group? Birbal said, 'Your Majesty, it was very simple. When I looked at you all, I noticed that those who were dressed like you but were not the real king had to constantly look at you for some clues how to act like a king. You were the only one who looked straight to the court assembly. There was no need for you to prove that you were a king. Naturally, you were very comfortable, but the phoney kings looked very nervous, because they were under tremendous pressure to appear like a king. I could clearly see the vast difference between your body language and theirs.' One who is truly in command does not need to look at others' faces, while others have to look at him all the time for guidance.

A highly confident, self-assured and genuine master never tries to steal the limelight. However, people's attention automatically gets riveted on him. His authority on meditation is based on his profound experiential understanding of the subject. He is highly self-assured because of the great wisdom he has earned through an in-depth study of meditation. He therefore requires no certificates from other people to establish his authority as a true master. It is quite self-evident that he has raised himself to a towering height of understanding and profound mastery over meditation. He doesn't need to make special efforts to put his extraordinary authority in meditation on display before others – his presence alone is enough to prove his calibre.

Other Qualities

A person fully immersed in meditation does not like to waste time in merely discussing meditation with people. He is not interested in needlessly exhausting himself by lecturing people on the importance of meditation. Instead, he prefers to remain in a state of meditation and keep enjoying it all the time.

Only when someone shows a genuine urge and curiosity to learn meditation does the master give guidance. Otherwise, instead of talking about meditation, he prefers to talk on other subjects. He never openly discloses his personal spiritual progress. For him, his meditative state is so precious that he never indulges in any idle talk about it and belittles it. A keen observer and a sincere practitioner of meditation can learn a great deal from the master's silence and quietness. What one needs to do is to develop an ability to read and understand the subtle messages hidden behind his profound stillness.

Those who are always engrossed in meditation prefer to remain in that state all the time. Unless persistently asked, they never speak about themselves. Their language is never bookish. Every single word they utter is a profound message by itself. But, one must know how to decipher meaning from such words. Their manner of speech is extremely simple and effortless. They never strive to convince others. They are so confident about their inner state that they are not concerned about proving their greatness to others. There isn't a trace of vanity in them: their self-confidence is of such a high order that it often astonishes onlookers.

It is safe to learn meditation from a true master who shows such inner qualities.

8

Make the Right Choice

We Have To Be Convinced

While choosing the master from whom we propose to take guidance in meditation and other aspects of spiritual growth, such as how to apply meditation in solving our day-to-day problems, we should not depend too heavily on external elements. If we get an opportunity to come closer to a person who is known for his spiritual mastery, we have to see how we feel in his company, with an open and unbiased mind. We have to make sure that we feel comfortable and at ease with him.

We should not regard any person as a master unless we are thoroughly convinced in our mind and heart about it. The mind and heart have their own ways of developing conviction. However, complete agreement and harmony between them is essential before we make any decision. If whatever is understood with the help of our intelligence is also acceptable to our heart, and vice versa, it becomes total acceptance.

Before embarking on the long voyage of meditation, we have to make sure that the master from whom we are going to learn the basics of meditation is acceptable to our mind and heart. If we do this right from the very first step we take on the path, we can avoid mistakes and make rapid progress in meditation.

It is better to get lost in the day-to-day material world and not learn meditation at all than to learn it under the improper guidance of an unsuitable spiritual master. Wisdom lies in being patient and waiting for a truly capable master to come along and guide us.

Making the Choice

In other areas of life, we can decide from whom we want to learn something, but in meditation it is different. We do not make a choice about our guru: he makes the choice for us. This arrangement makes a lot of sense to me, because, in our ignorance, we may make a wrong choice, but the guru, with his profound wisdom, is unlikely to make any mistakes. He is bound to be more correct in this regard. If he chooses us as his disciple, nothing else needs to be done. We have to just feel grateful to God and submit ourselves at the feet of such a master. He will take care of everything.

However, if we cannot accept him as he has accepted us, it is better to wait for some time than to submit in a haphazard manner. There is nothing wrong in rejecting a guru who has accepted us if we do not feel the same way about him. The great master Ramakrishna chose Vivekanand as his disciple, but Vivekanand did not accept him right away. He took some time before accepting Ramakrishna as his guru.

The major problem comes when a so-called guru starts saying that he has chosen his disciple. How do we know that the person who has made the decision is himself a real guru?

Dadu Maharaj and a Government Official

The following story is very meaningful in this context. Dadu Maharaj was a sage, well known for his spiritual wisdom. The area where Dadu lived was governed by a wicked government official who was notorious for his atrocities. The officer became very troubled due to a problem that he couldn't find a solution to, despite all his efforts to resolve it. While in a state of total turmoil, somebody advised him to go to Dadu Maharaj and seek his counsel to get peace of mind.

He immediately mounted his horse and went out in search of Dadu Maharaj. On his way, he came across a poor man who was removing stones and thorns from the road so as to prevent people walking on the path from getting hurt.

The official yelled at the poor man, 'You, tramp! Clear my way at once! Don't you know I am the chief government official of this area?'

The poor man looked at the official, smiled and quietly continued with his work. Seeing this, the officer became enraged like a bull. He completely lost his temper and lashed the poor man on his back with his whip, shoved him to the side of the road and moved on. After going quite some distance, he finally asked a passer-by about Dadu Maharaj. The officer realized that the poor man he had met on the road earlier was in fact the person he was looking for – it had been Dadu Maharaj himself! He felt ashamed of himself. 'How could I be so cruel to him? Why didn't I recognize him before I lashed out at him?' the official lamented.

Sheepishly, he went back to the poor man to beg his pardon and asked if he would still teach meditation to him.

Dadu Maharaj consoled him, 'Don't worry. I am not at all disturbed because of your bad behaviour towards me. On the contrary, I was amused at your cruelty. It certainly gave me an opportunity to test myself well. I could observe my reactions while you were insulting me. I know what you did was out of ignorance. If you want to learn meditation from somebody, you have to be extremely careful when making the choice. That is probably what you were doing unknowingly. Therefore, there is no reason for either of us to feel bad about the incident.'

The explanation thoroughly convinced the officer that Dadu Maharaj was undoubtedly the genuine spiritual master he was searching for, and decided to learn meditation under his able guidance.

SECRET NUMBER SIX

Find a Congenial Atmosphere Within Yourself

1

Significance of Outside Atmosphere

The quality of our meditation and our initial progress largely depends on the availability of a conducive atmosphere at home and outside. However, as we progress further and reach a certain level of maturity in meditation, we don't have to be so particular about such an atmosphere – we will be able to meditate anywhere, in any surroundings.

Significance of Outside Atmosphere

If we are novices in meditation, invariably our mind keeps wandering in all directions all the time. External disturbances may affect us and our meditation. It is therefore advisable to have one corner of a room in our apartment/house, or preferably a separate room, specially reserved for meditation practice. It is advisable to do nothing but meditation in that area. As far as possible, we have to consciously preserve the subtle vibrations of meditation in the atmosphere at home. Before we enter the meditation space or meditation room, we have to leave our shoes – along with all our worries and mundane thoughts – outside the special arena of meditation.

Put a soft, comfortable, thin mattress on the floor. Spread a clean white cotton sheet on it. Keep the lights dim. Wear soft, loose-fitting clothes. Burn an incense stick with a mild and calming fragrance. Make sure that there is enough fresh air, but not a direct breeze on your body.

Young Sapling of Meditation

In the early stages, we have to 'look after' our meditation as if we are taking care of a young sapling. We have to protect it from invaders, like people who do not approve of meditation or those who carry negative opinions about it. We should also be wary of those who are likely to make fun of us or those who are too materialistic in their approach towards life. They may make some negative comments or disparaging remarks and destroy the delicate sapling we have so carefully planted in the soil of our mind. Their remarks may disturb us so much that we may even impulsively feel like giving up the practice of meditation. That is why we should avoid such invaders and thus protect the sapling of meditation. Once it is capable of taking care of itself and has enough strength to protect itself, it will grow on its own. Special care will then no longer be necessary.

Gradual Weaning

We do the same thing with a growing child. For the first few months, it is entirely fed on mother's milk. Once it is four months old it is gradually weaned from breast milk. The process of weaning is kept slow, so that it allows adequate time for the child to adjust to the changing food pattern. We gradually go from liquid to solid food over a period of few weeks. The speed of weaning is adjusted according to child's capacity to take the change. Once the digestive power is properly developed, one can eat any food, anywhere, anytime provided it is wholesome, clean, pure, nutritious and fresh. We have to hold the hand of a small child while it is trying to learn how to write the alphabet. Once it is familiar with the art of writing, there is no need to hold its hands. Similarly, we have to observe care and concern with our meditation practice while we are not suitably self-sufficient in it. We have to gradually wean ourselves from the external anchorages and turn our vision inwards. Gradualness should be the key. When the weaning from external influences is gradual, we can easily adjust and accommodate the change. When the journey from the external to internal is slow, gentle and smooth, it is readily acceptable to us and further progress in meditation becomes easy.

After that, there is no need to worry about having a congenial external atmosphere, as we can create one within ourselves. Once we start enjoying meditation and are capable of doing it with utmost ease, the extraneous factors no longer matter to us. We can meditate anywhere, any time and that is precisely what is supposed to happen. Being particular about a proper atmosphere is essential when we are just beginners – being able to do it anywhere, any time is a sign of attaining maturity in our meditation.

Be Careful, Not Worried

However, we should never be too fussy or fastidious about a congenial atmosphere. A suitable atmosphere is certainly very helpful for meditation, but it is not everything. Moreover, it is quite possible that some people may not be that fortunate to enjoy the privilege of such an atmosphere. What should they do? Certainly they need not feel bad about it. They have to continue with the regular practice of meditation regardless of the available conditions.

Every day we have to take proper precautions before we start our meditation practice. We have to make sure that we are not disturbed by external factors. We may turn off the door bell, keep the phone receiver off the hook or cell-phone on silent mode, switch on the answering machine, hang a 'Do Not Disturb' sign on the door and so on. These arrangements help to avoid interruptions in the joy we experience in meditation. Once we get this joy, we know how precious it is for us.

It will be difficult to find a quiet place for meditation if we are living in a crowded and noisy city. Our neighbours may disturb us with the volume of their radios and TVs. But it is not worth getting upset or wasting too much time and energy in fighting against such odds. The best and most harmless solution is to change the time and place of our meditation practice.

If the problem still persists and the noise continues, our best bet is to use earplugs. The important thing is to do away with our problem and not to let it linger in our mind and disturb us. I know some sincere practitioners who practise meditation for two hours every day, while they are commuting in a crowded train in Mumbai, two hours each way to and from their work place. Those who have seen what it means to travel on a train in India can appreciate what I am saying.

Sometimes, we have no control over the situation. This problem frequently occurs during festival times in India. Indians have long been interested in religious festivals. Such festivals are held throughout the year. Many of them are celebrated publicly. Those foreigners who have visited India and have participated in the Holi or Ganesh festival will understand the point I am making. During such festive times, people construct temporary shades in the streets, put the festival idol of a god or goddess on a raised platform in this shade and offer group prayers to it. Usually, the group festivities start after office hours. Naturally, group prayers usually take place after meals, around 9.00 or 9.30 at night. During the prayers, loudspeakers are liberally used. Usually, they start with prayers on the loudspeakers, but often end up playing some popular movie songs! It is absurd to play such songs on the auspicious occasion of the festival. But these festivals are not just religious functions. They are for entertainment too. Considering the daily hard struggle for survival everybody has to go through, people always look forward to some kind of entertainment, at the end of the day. Going to a cinema is quite expensive. Very few can afford it. The only option is to make use of the festive time and combine prayers with some entertainment.

The problem often comes when we are finishing our busy schedule for the day and are about to start our meditation in the evening. We are then forced to listen to the high-volume music being played near our residence. It is extremely difficult to digest the situation.

Under the circumstances, we have to either talk our problem over with the organizers of such functions or keep ear plugs handy or if nothing else works, just stop our meditation for a day or two and simply enjoy the music. Why not? After all, it is a matter of choice. If we make up our minds we can enjoy anything and everything. We can continue to meditate, no matter what happens around us or just decide to enjoy the problem itself without any resistance at all.

This may seem like a sheepish, cowardly mentality, but it is not so. It is difficult to fight against something you don't like, more difficult to endure it and most difficult to live with it and enjoy it. Remember, the issue here is not of social reform or of proving to others how strong we are; but of finding a wise and immediate solution to a problem during meditation, so that we can continue to enjoy it better.

Fighting invariably breeds more fights and after the fight is over, the problem is still there and maybe it is even worse than before. In the process, a lot of time and energy gets wasted. It is therefore much wiser not to fight. 'No fighting' is not a matter of religious weakness, but a sign of great wisdom. Fighting that breeds fighting can never bring peace of mind. It keeps us upset and disturbed all the time.

Why waste our precious life in doing unwise things? Why not quietly accept the reality as it is, and learn to live with it? Why not use the same time and energy for meditation and for developing insight into the process of bringing meditation into our daily living?

During meditation, if we confront a difficult or an inevitable situation where we can't do anything to create a congenial atmosphere around us, there is no point wasting our precious time cursing or blaming others or the circumstances or us for not having the right conditions. It will be a sheer waste of time and energy. It is much better and wiser to quietly accept the reality as it is, and learn to live with it.

Sometimes, our meditation gets disturbed due to difficult mundane problems that have no immediate solution in sight. In such situations, we should stop our meditation and remain tuned into the problem to witness its effects on us. Thus, we can understand and solve it more easily. We will be less upset and irritable too.

2

Atmosphere at Home

For meditation to be fruitful, the family atmosphere should be free, friendly and playful. I know some practitioners of meditation who assume that because they are doing a spiritual activity, they are entitled to behave with a lack of consideration for others. They make the life of other members of their family very difficult because of their whims and idiosyncrasies.

We have to bear in mind that as far as possible we should not cause any nuisance to our family. There is no need to have grandiose ideas about ourselves just because we are practising meditation. We have to be simple and accommodating in our approach in order to create a good atmosphere at home. It is easy at home to make the necessary arrangements to meet our physical needs for comfort while meditating, but far more challenging to win the understanding of our family members that meditation is a welcome guest in the family.

Initially it is better to keep meditation to ourselves and not let everybody know about it. Just stay focused on a regular and uninterrupted practice. Let the family observe some change in our behaviour and in us. There is no need to talk about the benefits of meditation all the time. Let our life speak louder than our words. Until it happens, it is better to keep quiet and observe patience. Once they see some positive change in us, they will automatically feel more inclined to take advice from us. Even if they don't, they will at least realize the true worth of meditation. Naturally, they will co-operate with us more easily. If it appears that our family is genuinely interested in learning meditation, we may share our knowledge with them at a later stage when we have really mastered it ourselves. Until that time, there is no point in giving lessons prematurely.

Family Background

Family atmosphere to some extent depends on our family background too, that is the family in which we were born. How did our parents rear us? Did both parents or only one parent raise us? How was the atmosphere at home during our childhood? Was it friendly and free of tensions or far too disciplinarian? If our family background favoured spiritual practices and philosophical learning, naturally it is going to be very easy for us to understand, practise and do well in meditation.

If both parents are medical doctors, for example, we will be exposed to a medical-related atmosphere at home, right from our childhood. If we decide to go for a medical career ourselves later, we will have the added advantage of this family background. If appropriate, we can get guidance from our parents during our career.

If we have a family business, we will get the opportunity to know everything about how a business is run. We will be familiar with the nature of problems related to the handling of the business. We will also know how to manage various problems during bad and good times; how to get a feel of the changing market trends; how to develop proper plans to exploit the market fluctuations; how to strike a balance between manufacturing and sales activities and so on. We will have direct access to practical training and knowledge about successful management of a business, which will surely be far more important and useful than knowledge one gets from books on business management. Under such conditions, it will also be very easy for us to start and run a new business of our choice and do it very successfully, too.

Don't Feel Bad or Proud

Similarly, if we have a family background of meditation, we will find it easy to meditate. However, we obviously do not have any conscious control over where we are going to be born in this life. So we need not waste our valuable time complaining about not being born into a family with a good spiritual background. It will be wiser to spend that time on moving on from the problem. As this is not going to change in our lifetime, why worry about it? Why not accept the reality and do something concrete about taking proper care of our present problems? That will help us more in meditation than anything else. We need not feel ashamed if we don't have a good family background, nor should we feel proud if we are fortunate to have one.

During my college days, I was an active member of an organization working for the rights and welfare of youth. One day, during an important meeting, one of the officers of the organization introduced me to a newly joined group of young students. He said, 'He is Samprasad Vinod. He is in S. P. College. I know that he will not approve of his introduction, as the youngest son of Maharshi Vinod.'

In reply, I said, 'I think it was an incomplete introduction. I am Samprasad Vinod, but at the same time I am also the youngest son of Maharshi Vinod, and I do not feel ashamed of being introduced as his son. My father hasn't done anything so sinful that I should feel obliged to abandon my relationship with him or his name. At my age, I have not achieved anything so great that I should make a sovereign claim on my individual identity. I am also aware that just being his son is by itself not my achievement. I don't see any reason to feel proud about it either. I only feel grateful to say the least. I am very clear that I am still in the making and haven't made it yet.'

Don't Get Caught in the Web

It is possible that our present incarnation is determined by our deeds from the past life. The theory of Karma is one of the best explanations of the riddle of birth and rebirth. But it is difficult to ascertain the authenticity of this theory purely on rational grounds, because there is an element of subjectivity in it. It is true that through the process of regression we can 'look back' into a past life and learn about our past incarnations. But it is not possible for everybody to do that.

Many people believe in the process of incarnation, simply because some person in authority has told them to do so. But that doesn't solve the riddle. It is really not necessary to get caught in theories about past life, life after death and reincarnation; because whatever was or were our previous incarnation/s, the fact still remains that we are here in this world, in the present life.

As far as our progress on the path of meditation or spiritual evolution is concerned, it hardly matters where we came from in a past life. What is more important is how we make use of the present life and work our way to striking a balance between worldly and spiritual life. We should always remember that any journey, whether it is small or big, whether it is in the inner world or outer, starts from where we actually are – it cannot start from an imaginary starting point.

So too the journey of meditation starts from where we actually are. This means it should start from this life. If we haven't experientially ascertained the authenticity of our previous incarnation, posthumous existence and reincarnation, they are nothing more than imaginary mystical states for us. Under such circumstances, it is much wiser to ignore these states and focus our attention on the practice of meditation. There is absolutely no point in building the superstructure of meditation on the weak foundation of imagination.

SECRET NUMBER SEVEN

*Grow Beyond Dreams
and Desires*

1

Differentiate between Meditation and Sleep

Many people ask me a very interesting question, which can appear quite logical. If dissolution of the mind is what we have to achieve through meditation, and we can do this in deep sleep, why should we go through the long process of learning and practising meditation?

Similar State, Different Process

It is true that the 'no-thought state' of meditation appears similar to deep sleep, but there is a world of difference in the manner in which we reach this state. The most striking difference is the presence of awareness in meditation and its total absence during sleep, a distinction that is quite self-evident.

At a superficial level sleep appears easier than meditation, because we think that it is under our control. To some extent it is, but not entirely. Meditation appears very difficult in the beginning, but eventually it turns out to be easy, because it is our very nature.

Sometimes, while studying or doing some important work, we may have to drink a cup of coffee or tea to help us stay awake during the night. But beyond a certain point, it becomes impossible to remain awake and alert. If we insist on staying awake, in spite of the uncontrollable urge to sleep, we struggle to whip ourselves into action. We cannot however continue with such self-torture for a long time – when we reach our limit, we are overtaken by sleep, whether we like it or not. If we do not listen to nature's hints or do not respond to its demands, we have to pay the price. If the late nights continue, we suffer from acidity, headache, irritability, lack of concentration, memory lapses and so on.

We are of course free to believe that we don't care about nature. But, it doesn't make any difference to nature. It never changes its course and the events that follow also do not change.

The message is – sleep is natural and it should be so. We can never win over anything that is natural, particularly on a long-term basis. Occasional victory over natural sleep is only temporary, and natural sleep always prevails in spite of our best efforts to control it.

Sound Sleep is Useful for Meditation

It is quite natural to feel physically and mentally tired at the end of a busy working day. Feeling sleepy at night after a busy day is natural. Not taking heed of a genuine need to sleep is the most foolish thing to do. If we have to stay awake working late nights at home, it really means that we are not able to manage our time properly.

That is why we have to learn to manage our time better and welcome sleep after a long tiring day at the office. Anyway, if we are really tired there will be hardly any choice but to sleep, whether we want to or not. As we all know, sleep works very effectively if it is taken at the right time and in the right amount. It is essential for our health and wellbeing. It acts as a tonic to the tired organs of our body. After proper sleep, we feel refreshed and energized to meet the challenges of life more effectively and efficiently.

The wakeful alertness that follows sound sleep is helpful in meditation. It improves the quality of self-awareness. If we do not allow ourselves enough rest before meditation, reaching higher states of consciousness will be very difficult.

Meditation Improves Sleep

As much as good sleep can improve meditation, meditation can also improve the quality of our sleep. Good sleep obviously means sound sleep, and sound sleep means dreamless sleep. During sound sleep, the mind is completely silent, as if dissolved into nothingness.

Dissolution of the mind means dissolution of all thoughts, dreams and the interplay of illusions during the dream state. If we want to be free of dreams during sleep, we have to learn how to stop dreaming during the day.

Meditation brings radical transformation and revolution in the inner world. The very foundation of our life gets completely changed. The world of imagination and dreams is now replaced by the actual, real world. Dreams during sleep are only extensions of the daydream world when we are awake during the day. As we make progress in meditation, our daydreaming is significantly reduced. As the daydreaming is minimized, its extension during sleep is also proportionately decreased. Consequently, the number of dreams during sleep are also substantially reduced.

Eventually, the daydreaming stops completely. Its extension in the form of sleep-dreams also comes to an end – our usual sleep is made completely dream-free. Dream-free sleep provides deep and profound rest. Over a period of time, we realize that our sleep requirement is drastically reduced, while the quality of sleep is substantially improved.

2

Why Do We Dream?

By knowing why and how we dream, we can be free of dreams. Being free of dreams means being closer to the 'no-thought state' we are trying to reach through meditation.

Are Dreams Necessary?

Modern psychologists say that dreams are necessary. In one sense this is true. While living in this complex world, we have to relate to so many people and deal with so many complicated situations. While doing so, many things do not happen the way we want them to happen. Often, there is nothing that we can do about it.

An impoverished person may have to sacrifice many of his aspirations, because he has no money to satisfy those desires. He has to suppress many of his longings, do a lot of things against his wishes and face constant disappointment regarding the trivial pleasures in life. All this leads to tremendous frustration, turmoil and distress. It is impossible to release this pressure. He cannot give free expression to his desires, emotions, thoughts and feelings during the day as he has to work hard to make his living. But during sleep, there is no need for such restraint. He is his own master during sleep. He is free to imagine whatever he desires. Naturally, during sleep, he tends to give full expression to his unfulfilled desires through wonderful dreams. He is free to imagine that he is the richest person in the world. Nobody can prevent him from having such a dream. It is his sovereign territory, where he is in command of everything, the supreme boss.

Through dreams, he seeks the imaginary satisfaction of being a rich and important person, something which is denied to him during waking hours. False satisfaction through dreams reduces the unbearable stress of daily living to bearable limits. Although temporary, dreams can be a great relief for a person who has to face the hardships of mundane living. A temporary relief from such suffering is certainly a solace.

Being poor is not necessarily just material poverty. It could be mental, emotional or intellectual poverty as well. In this sense we are all poor to one degree or another and therefore we all need dreams to give vent to our unfulfilled desires.

According to some scientists, everybody dreams during sleep. They say it is impossible not to dream and those who claim that they don't are mistaken.

In a way, dreaming is harmful too. By encouraging dreaming, we can get into a bad habit of paying more attention to an imaginary world than the real – we get disconnected from the concrete realities of day-to-day living. An 'imaginary' solution to a 'real' problem may not always be an appropriate solution. By giving importance to dreaming, we slowly reduce our ability to face real problems. We may get some clues about solving our problems through our dreams, but apart from that how can the world of imagination rescue us from the problems of the real world?

Attraction Of Social Dreams

Very few people can live without dreams. Most of us actually thrive on dreams. Children dream of being grown-ups, so that they can do things as they like, without any restrictions. Adults relive the innocent, stress-free life of their childhood memories in their dreams. Some of those who are single look forward to getting married and some who are married eagerly await the court order for divorce. For most people therefore, living in the dream world is almost a necessity!

The clever politicians know how to make the most of this common need and be successful in politics. They first convert it into a weakness and then exploit it to their advantage.

Mrs Indira Gandhi, the former Prime Minister of India succeeded in doing this in one election. She knew that she had to win over the electorate, so she offered them a 'promise of wonderland' and marketed her ideas well. People started believing in what she said. For a charismatic person like her, it wasn't too difficult to do the rest.

She chose 'Garibi Hatao', or 'Eradicate Poverty', as her campaign slogan to attract the masses. It brought her to power with a huge landslide victory. She managed to shift their focus from their own problems to a well-projected dream world, bringing her an historic victory.

She knew that it was not easy to eradicate poverty from India. But who was interested in such eradication except the real poor? Elections were over, poverty continued, public euphoria subsided. The masses became disillusioned and subsequently removed her from power in the following elections.

Filmmakers also use the same trick. They sell dreams to the gullible and keep them engaged in dreaming. Ironically, those who watch the dream of prosperity remain poor while the filmmakers who show the dreams make lots of money.

It is very interesting to see that most people who are unable to cope with the harsh day-to-day realities of life usually prefer to listen to those who offer them dreams. They do not know how to solve their problems, but seldom want to do anything concrete about it. They often dislike genuine well-wishers who want to show them the 'real' way – spiritual masters can make them aware of the actual truth, but most people are seldom interested in such truths.

Most people like to remain absorbed in their own world of dreams. They survive on the false hope that, although their present condition is not so good, it will be better in a few years and eventually everything will be fine.

Who can help those who have made up their minds to live in a dream world? They act according to their individual choices.

Suppose you are sitting with your friend, who is thoroughly absorbed in watching the unreal world depicted in a movie. If you remind him of the falsity of the world that is being projected on the screen, he does not want to hear that from you. If you continue in what you are saying he will not approve of it. If you still persist with your efforts to bring him out of the imaginary world, most certainly you will lose a good friend. How can he leave something that he likes so much? It is next to impossible for him to do that. For such people, it hardly matters whether you show them dreams or not – they will find dreams anyway and remain absorbed in those dreams.

We may therefore say that dreams are necessary and useful for some people who are under unbearable pressures in the real world. For them, dreaming serves as an outlet and a safety valve through which excess inner pressure is released.

It is a temporary relief but, nevertheless, it surely is a welcome relief for them. After some of the pressure is relieved, they may start thinking more clearly. They may also review their situation and start looking for a 'dream-free' life.

3

Freedom from Desires is Freedom from Dreams

It is true that most people do need dreams to help relieve them of the stresses of day-to-day living. But dreams provide only a temporary relief from such stress.

However, a realized and enlightened soul can clearly see and understand the illusion of life and also of dreams. He is wide awake to the all-pervasive insecurity and worthlessness of life as a whole. He is himself securely grounded in worldly as well as spiritual wisdom, and has expanded and grown in his awareness. Such a person can easily transcend dreams and go beyond them. It is quite natural for a person who has permanently transcended all desires and yearnings within his life to be free of dreams.

A king dreams of being a beggar. When he gets up from his slumber, he calls on his guru. The king tells him about the dream that he just had and seeks his counsel, 'Sir, I am really confused. Will you please remove my confusion? Please explain to me whether the "king" had a short dream of being a beggar or a "beggar" is having a long dream of being a king? Who among the two is real, the beggar or the king?' The guru answers, 'Both the king as well as beggar are false.' The learned guru could tell this, because he himself was free of all bondage. He knew that the world we live in and the imaginary dream world are both unreal.

Chain of Desires
There is a beautiful Sanskrit saying that describes 'desire' as the most peculiar of all kinds of chains in this world. A person who is 'chained'

to it keeps running after the fulfilment of one desire after another, and the one who is 'released' from this chain becomes incapacitated like a cripple. I love this saying, because it describes the working of desire in the most meaningful and precise manner.

We know that someone who is bound in an iron chain becomes completely immobile and cannot move from one place to another. But as soon as he is unchained, the same person can move anywhere quite swiftly and without any difficulty.

Desire is such a mental shackle that a person who is bound in it continuously tries to do something to fulfil the desire. But a realized person, who is totally and permanently free of all the mental chains of desire, becomes completely still. After being released from the shackles of desire, there is nothing left to be done or achieved in this life or in this world for him. He remains forever immersed in inner bliss. He experiences profound peace of mind and lasting inner stability. Paradoxically, all his desires are automatically and permanently fulfilled, by virtue of his being free of them all.

It is quite interesting to see that those who are governed by desires keep running after fulfilment and a person who is permanently free of all desires enjoys complete fulfilment and satisfaction without doing anything.

Creation, Fulfilment and Resurrection of Desires

It is our usual experience that fulfilment of one desire creates others that are connected with the original desire. We start satisfying the newly created desires, which in turn creates a new batch of related desires. The process continues endlessly and we keep running after fulfilment of one desire after another.

Some of the desires do not get adequate attention or they become outdated over a period of time. Such desires remain dormant for some time, but as soon as a favourable climate is present they get resurrected in different forms. Some dormant desires flourish into new desires, when they get proper attention and a favourable atmosphere.

Whether it is before, after or without fulfilment, desires appear, stay around for some time, disappear or get resurrected, depending on the availability of a suitable climate for such rejuvenation. The cycle gets repeated all the time.

Most of us spend all our lives fulfilling one desire after another, getting completely trapped in an ever-expanding web of desires. Most of us get thoroughly exhausted in the end, without achieving anything like real fulfilment. Most people die with a bundle of unfulfilled desires, which are supposedly carried into the next life.

After spending many years studying this never-ending cycle of desires, one gets really intrigued by the nature of this cycle.

The Quest Begins

At this point, one starts asking fundamental questions such as: What am I doing this for? I have been trying to satisfy my desires, but I am creating more and more desires every day. By the time I feel that I have fulfilled one desire and achieved something, I see a new generation of desires waiting around the corner. What am I going to achieve through this running around? How long am I going to continue with this madness? How long am I going to run after this unending chain of desires? Is there any way out of this problem?

These kinds of thoughts may creep into our mind every once in a while, but we seldom realize their genuine importance. They are certainly very difficult thoughts to pursue, particularly when there isn't sufficient guidance or wise counsel available to us. We may quickly lose interest, stop the quest, start running away from those thoughts, and once again get lost in the ever-growing mesh of desires.

By doing so, we lose the golden opportunity to understand our desires and thus go beyond them.

Don't Stop the Quest

We may also think that we have to go through lots of hardships for the fulfilment of desires, and yet they do not get fully satisfied. As such, the permanent satisfaction of desires is like a distant dream. Why then should we pursue yet another far-off fantasy of going beyond dreams?

One may also rationalize and say that, however false and fake the world of desires may be, at least something concrete seems to happen there. Moreover, who knows what is going to happen after being free of all desires? Is it really worth working towards that? One may also feel that it is much better to be on a familiar path than to take any chances.

It is not possible to find answers to such questions unless our thinking is supplemented by doing something concrete, in the form of meditation. In the absence of such an option, one naturally takes a conventional approach to those questions and once again gets lost in a self-perpetuating web of desires.

In fact, we are really fortunate to have such questions. It is a great opportunity. Therefore, we have to be wise to make the most of such a chance.

First of all, we have to supplement our thoughts with much deeper reflection on the issue. We have to realize that our mind gets more restless and agitated if we run after the fulfilment of our desires. Consequently, it becomes more difficult to silence it and to turn it towards meditation. Thus, running after desires is actually very harmful for our growth in meditation.

At this juncture, it is therefore worthwhile to study how to get total freedom from our desires.

4

Freedom from Desires
is a Mental State

We have to clearly understand that being free of desires and cravings is not merely a physical act, but involves freedom from desires at a mental level too. If we develop better understanding and deeper insight into the entire process of living, it will be easy for us to be free of our desires.

Every craving creates bondage, and bondage is the basic cause of our suffering. To be free of suffering, we have to know how to be free of every type of mental imprisonment. We can't be free of our desires unless we are free of their bondage. We can't achieve such freedom if we constantly wage a war against our desires. In contrast to popular belief, fighting against desires is not the real solution to this problem.

If fighting is not the real solution, then what is the alternative? If we go on fulfilling our desires one after another all the time, that continues to create a great deal of disturbance and turmoil in us because we will never feel satisfied in the end. So what is the remedy for this problem?

Know your Desires

My father was a great spiritual master. He used to say, 'Discovering the binding nature of a desire is by itself a true liberation from its bondage.' I think he was absolutely right.

If we closely observe our desires and try to find out how they come into being and enslave us, the bondage disappears immediately. We don't need to do anything more than that. We have to just keep our mind open and go on studying how every desire gets manifested and in the process creates bondage. We have to also study the details of its expression. Thus, we can clearly grasp its enslaving nature.

If we just study one desire thoroughly and in great depth, it helps us develop insight into the basic realities of life. After this exercise is over, we emerge more sensible and mature than before. After that, we won't run after every desire. We won't be unduly disturbed if for some reason a particular desire is not satisfied. Gradually, with continuous self-study we grow in our wisdom. This wisdom is useful in other areas of life too.

Over a period of time, we can clearly understand and also completely accept the truth that we are not going to get true satisfaction, real joy and lasting peace of mind by getting carried away with our desires. Consequently, all the agonies and frustrations associated with the fulfilment of desires as well as those with unfulfilled desires permanently come to an end.

When we are left with no desire to fulfil our desires, it may seem like a downbeat state. On the face of it, it does look like ordinary pessimism, but in reality it is vastly different.

Someone who has given up all his desires truly lives life to its full potential. He enjoys immense joy, profound satisfaction and absolute peace of mind. Such a person would not waste his time and energy in running after pleasures or happiness. They would come to him uninvited. After having experienced this state, one begins to lead a very comfortable, carefree and effortless life.

Transcending Desires

Being free of desires really means going beyond them or transcending their inbuilt limitations. We do occasionally experience such transcendence with some of our desires naturally.

As a child, all of us must have liked to play one game or another. I used to love flying kites. But now that I am grown up, I don't have to take a vow and say, 'Come what may, I am not going to fly kites from tomorrow.' There is absolutely no need to do that, because now, as an adult, kites have no attraction left for me. My interests have changed over the years. So I don't have to put in any extra effort to stop flying kites.

If I decide to fly a kite with my son or nephew, it will be because the child is interested in it. It will not have much appeal for me but I will do it because it makes the child happy.

Fulfilment of Desires after Transcendence

There is a world of difference between fulfilment of desires before going beyond them and afterwards. Before transcendence, we are worried and concerned about fulfilling our desires, because our happiness in life largely depends on such fulfilment. But after transcendence, we can 'play' with our desires like we play with our children.

While playing with our children, we do not get disturbed if we start losing the game. We also do not get elated if we begin to win. The child may get upset if they lose and excited if they win. We may join the child in the sorrow of failure as well as the joy of success. But deep down, neither losing nor winning will have any effect on us.

We do not get affected because we are grown up and have crossed the boundaries of the joy of childhood. Not that we are less joyful than the child with whom we are playing, but our reasons and reference points for being joyful are completely different from his.

Childishness of the Grown-Ups

We often come across people who are grown-up in age, but not in wisdom and maturity. Physically, it seems that they have grown out of their childhood but deep down nothing has really changed. They play the same childish games, except that the manner in which they play those games has changed. Now their needs are different. They like to play with different toys such as money, power and position. These 'grown-up kids' get completely absorbed in playing with their toys, just as small children do.

While playing with those toys they forget everything else that is happening around them. Like small children, the grown-up kids become mad with excitement when they win and are broken when they lose. As long as they are winning the game, everything is fine. But the moment they start losing, they get upset. They play all sorts of tricks to protect their small egos from getting hurt.

They usually blame their failure on other players, friends, the playground, the opposition team and so on. In short they blame everybody and everything else except themselves.

Behaviour after Freedom from Desires

If we study one of our desires thoroughly and completely, we will be free of its bondage. If we are free of the bondage, we will be able to satisfy our desire more easily. Our mind will be fully available to go through the experience of fulfilling our desire. Naturally, we will 'enjoy' the same object of desire more. When I use the term 'enjoy', I do not mean 'excitement'. I am referring to a very different kind of joy, which is strikingly different from excitement, but it is still as joyful as any other joy.

Once we understand what is meant by true satisfaction of a desire, our whole outlook towards life is completely changed. After that, whether we are in possession of an object for the satisfaction of a particular desire or not, will not make any difference to us. The presence or absence of the object will not disturb our mental state.

After we have studied one desire thoroughly, in the same manner we can study other desires too. Every time we do such study, we realize that proper knowledge and understanding of a desire is the only sure way of going beyond that desire.

A person who has done this with all his desires becomes permanently free of their bondage. His behaviour may appear very similar to any other person, but internally he is different. His inner stability and equilibrium remains unaffected under all circumstances. Sometimes, we may find him doing the same things as other people, but that does not mean he is like them. In fact, willingness to mix with other people and do whatever they are doing is the real sign of being an extraordinary person.

For a person who knows all existence to be an illusion, it is highly unlikely that he would ever get caught up in trivial dreams, as there is absolutely no need for him to do that.

In movies we see flashbacks. Sometimes, two or three flashbacks come in a row and we are not able to make out where one flashback ended and another started. But a filmmaker who is conversant with the filmmaking process can spot it with utmost precision.

Life is also like a series of flashbacks. Most of us may not be able to know where the dream of our present life began. But a person who sees existence as nothing but a drama or a film would never face this problem.

In short, we may say that a person who is half-asleep and half-awake during daytime is bound to like dreams. He is obviously going to keep watching and enjoying dreams, one way or another. But one who is wide awake in the true sense, during wakeful times as well as awake during sleep, who knows that life is nothing but a long dream, gets enlightened after such knowledge. For him, dreaming and dreams become irrelevant. One must remember that being awake during sleep is not a self-contradiction: it means being deeply interested in exploring the truth about slumber, something that continues without our conscious knowledge about it.

How can a person who is permanently liberated from a state of natural slumber as well as the slumber of ignorance ever dream? After all, one has to be asleep to have dreams.

SECRET NUMBER EIGHT

*Be Creative at Worldly
and Spiritual Levels*

1

Dreams and Creativity – A Psychological Perspective

When understanding dreams, we have to know the meaning of psychological creativity. Through psychological creativity, we can take care of our day-to-day problems more effectively. If we handle our worldly problems well, they stop disturbing us. As a result, the intensity and number of problems get substantially reduced to a manageable level. Naturally, it proves useful in improving the quality of our meditation practice.

Psychologists often say that there is nothing wrong in daydreaming and letting our minds drift a little bit. They recommend 'purposeful dreaming' for improving creativity. During specially designed training programs on psychological creativity, the participants are encouraged to develop their power of creative imagination.

Power of Imagination and Dreaming

Firstly, we have to understand the difference between the power of imagination and dreaming. While dreaming, we are far removed from reality. Dreaming is not a conscious and purposeful act of creative imagination. The power of imagination, however, can be extremely useful for solving our problems.

There is a definite logic behind using the power of imagination for problem solving. If we approach any given problem with a prejudiced mind, we will only get a stereotypical answer to it, which cannot be a real answer. Such answers are not useful for solving our problems.

Every problem is unique, so we cannot afford to approach it with a prejudiced mind, otherwise we may get an answer that is an outcome of our prejudice rather than the right answer. Naturally, such an answer can never be a real and lasting solution.

Brainstorming

While working on a given problem, if we let our mind run free completely, we can brainstorm without any difficulty. Brainstorming essentially means creative imagination.

During a session on creative imagination, we are supposed to temporarily suspend all the extraneous controls over our mind, let go completely and allow all thoughts to emerge without any resistance or hindrance. Then we are expected to write down all the answers that come to mind, without any analysis or censorship. We need not even worry about whether they are right answers or wrong.

After the session is over, we end up with a long list of possible solutions to our problem. Now we have to pick the solutions that are most appropriate for the problem we are facing. We have to examine the solutions further, to decide which among them is the best solution, which is the second best, and so on until we have a prioritized list of solutions. Then we have to go through a phase of complete relaxation, before we conclude the brainstorming session.

Free Play of Imagination and Reality

The power of imagination is a powerful asset when it is properly utilized for finding creative solutions to our problems. But if it leads us into a negative mode of thinking, it is likely to be very harmful for our growth and wellbeing.

If our session on free imagination is followed by daydreaming, it is highly detrimental to us. Our mind may get flooded with thoughts like, 'What will happen if I do this?', 'What will happen if I do that?', 'What will I do if I do not succeed?' or 'How will I celebrate my success?' It is like building wonderful castles in the air. What is the use of such castles if they are not built on a solid foundation of reality? They will have no value or use. However, if we do not waste our time in daydreaming and make proper use of our power of imagination, it will help us find creative solutions to our problems.

Abraham Lincoln once said, 'If you want to be successful, keep your head above the clouds and feet firmly grounded on the floor.' This means that one should be bold enough to think big about scaling the highest peaks of achievement in life. But, while doing so, one should never forget the basic realities of life.

In other words, our power of imagination must go hand in hand with the actual hard work we have to do to achieve great success in life. If we want to make our dreams come true, mere daydreaming will not be sufficient. We will have to ensure that our dreams concur with the factual realities of life. If we lose our contact with the ground, there is every possibility of endlessly drifting in the dream world of imagination. Moreover, the power of imagination or psychological creativity cannot improve if we keep dreaming about something all the time.

In conclusion, we may say that well-directed, focused and conscious dreaming is known as the free play of imagination. In contrast, the usual sort of dreaming is a wild, uncontrolled and unconscious display of the power of imagination.

Well-directed dreaming is primarily useful in the worldly life and indirectly useful in meditation.

2

Spontaneity of Spiritual Creativity

Uniqueness of Spiritual Creativity

Regular practice of meditation improves psychological creativity. Psychological creativity helps us understand and solve many problems in day-to-day life. Our worldly life becomes less stressful and less problematic. The quality of meditation improves in proportion to the improving psychological creativity and improving day-to-day life. Once the quality of meditation improves, spontaneous expression of spiritual creativity begins.

The philosophical contemplation and reflection of the seers and sages can be considered as the most exalted manifestations of spiritual creativity. The towering heights of spiritual literature produced by the seers are essentially a combined effect of the power of imagination and an experiential knowledge of the inner world. Both these powers reach the highest level of perfection in the sages and seers.

Dnyaneshwar, one of the greatest seers from the state of Maharashtra in India, wrote a classic commentary on the *Bhagavad Gita* called *Dnyaneshwari*. *Bhagavad Gita* is an enlightening dialogue between the warrior Arjuna and Lord Krishna during the battle between Kauravas, as the bad guys on one side and Pandavas as the good guys on the other. The main treatise is written in Sanskrit, which is difficult to understand for the common man. Having noticed this problem, the great seer Dnyaneshwar, driven by empathy for the general populace, wrote a commentary, known as *Dnyaneshwari*, on *Bhagavad Gita* in the local language.

After the divine experience of the highest state of consciousness, or *samadhi*, he developed great love and deep concern for the wellbeing of the whole of existence. Profound compassion flowed in the form of spiritual creativity and was expressed as the outstanding scripture popularly known as *Dnyaneshwari*. It is one of the most profound, lucid and beautiful commentaries on the *Gita*. The outpouring of spiritual creativity continued after completion of *Dnyaneshwari* and was expressed in several other wonderful treatises on yoga philosophy and spiritual life that he wrote later.

This great man left his mortal body more than 700 years ago while he was sitting in a deep state of *samadhi*. People still remember, worship and adore him and his literature: hundreds of thousands of people still follow his teaching and derive great benefits from it.

Limitations of Worldly Creativity

Once we understand what is meant by spiritual creativity, we can easily understand and appreciate the difference between worldly and spiritual creativity. One of the hallmarks of worldly creativity is its focus on 'usefulness'. It is the prime consideration behind all that comes under worldly creativity.

As we all know, some industrial corporations encourage and promote what are known as 'suggestion boxes'. If anybody working in the company comes up with an innovative idea about improving the product of the company or its working, he or she is supposed to write down his/her idea on a piece of paper and put it into the box. The box is opened every week or every month, depending on how full it is. All the suggestions are read and discussed in a group meeting. If a particular idea is really useful, it is usually accepted, implemented and ultimately incorporated in the working of the company. The person who thought of the idea receives a handsome prize as a token of appreciation for his/her contribution.

This concept is quite popular in the corporate world because it is very useful in solving different problems related to different areas of an organization.

There is nothing wrong in making use of the creative talents of people in this manner. But the motive behind such creativity is usually reduced to its potential usefulness to the person who receives the prize and the company which benefits from his contribution.

It may, however, prove harmful for the overall growth of that person. Once the specific application of the innovative idea is over, he/she may go through a stage of stagnation in creativity. The innovative solution one has offered to a given problem becomes stale after a time. It remains useful only in a limited context, for a limited period of time and at a specific place within the company where it is being used. This kind of creativity is useful in solving certain industry-specific problems – it can never enjoy the privilege of universal application and use.

Manifestations Differ, Underlying Life Energy Remains the Same

Spiritual creativity is far more spontaneous than material creativity. We can never develop such creativity with a utilitarian motive in mind. It manifests on its own, after realization of the ultimate truth. The highest truth is eternally beyond all restrictions of time, place and person. Realization of the highest truth is the same as revelation of the all-pervasive life principle residing in all the 'existential units' of this creation. It comprises all living creatures, plants, animals and humans as well as apparently non-living objects like oceans, mountains, rocks, stones, soil and rivers. The life principle remains the same everywhere.

Essentially, there is no qualitative difference in the 'level of life' or 'aliveness' among different creatures from this universe. It may appear to manifest differently in different parts of creation, but their basic factual existence – or what we can call their 'beingness' – remains the same for all. The difference is only in the particulars, not in the substance.

The life principle found in a man residing in London is neither more nor less than a person residing in the USA. As this principle is equally distributed in all parts of our body, we cannot say that our legs are more alive than our hands or the other way round. We cannot say that a 15-year-old boy is more alive than a 70-year-old person. A 15-year-old boy certainly appears more energetic than the old person does. But the difference between them is only at a manifest level. 'Aliveness' is the same in both, but there is a difference in the manifestation of this aliveness through their bodies. A young body is more capable of giving full expression to the aliveness than the old body can and therefore the young person appears more full of energy than the old person does. But the quality and quantity of the life energy remains the same in both.

In the same manner, the manifestation of aliveness is different in different objects that constitute this universe. The manifestation of aliveness is relative in nature and it varies with respect to time, place and person. But at a pure existential level, it remains the same. Its distribution is also the same everywhere.

Lasting Value of Spiritual Creativity

The experiential realization of individual life energy and universal life energy brings about a radical transformation in our attitude towards life. After such realization, for example, Dnyaneshwar went into a state of spiritual creativity, which flowed through him in the form of classic spiritual literature. After the highest experience of *samadhi*, whatever Dnyaneshwar said or did became a holy offering of selfless service to the whole of existence as well as God.

In contrast to this, material creativity, which is nurtured on utilitarian motives, has no lasting value. It remains useful in the context of a particular situation or a specific problem. It becomes redundant once its usefulness is over.

Patanjali, the greatest of all the yogis, created a monumental scripture on yoga, known as the *Yoga Sutras of Patanjali*. He never worried about getting his treatise on yoga published. He was not worried about the book being liked by people or making enough profits for himself or for his publisher. His book was not an ordinary contemporary book. It was a very special kind of book – a scripture on yoga. The scriptures do not have any superficial entertainment value: their 'value' lies in being 'invaluable'. Scriptures are meant for spiritual enlightenment and nothing less than that.

The *Yoga Sutras of Patanjali* were composed about 400 CE, but it is still very useful to millions of practitioners of yoga living in all parts of the world. It is eternally invaluable, which is why it has crossed all man-made national and geographical boundaries and religious barriers to become such an internationally acclaimed treasure of human understanding and wisdom. It is not a sovereign property of India, but a precious heritage of all humanity.

3

What Is More Important – Manifest Creativity or Unmanifest Ability?

Being Creative is Enough

One peculiarity of spiritual creativity is that it may or may not be manifested in the form of a tangible result or product. It is enough to be in a state of such creativity, though – there is absolutely no need to try anything special to express it in a tangible way.

A famous author who was also a critic once went to meet J. Krishnamurti. While introducing himself to Krishnamurti, he said he was an author and a poet. Krishnamurti asked him, 'Is it necessary for a poet to write poems?' The famous author had no answer to this basic question. He was completely flabbergasted. A question like this had never occurred to him in his life.

Human history has seen many saints and seers who were well known for the substantial contributions they have made to human understanding and wellbeing through their literature. But there must have been an equal number of lesser-known seers and sages who were in every other respect comparable except that they did not create any tangible literature. But just because they did not create any literature does not mean that they were not as spiritually evolved as those who did. They could also have had the same creative ability, except that it was not expressed in the form of any literature. Maybe their role in the overall scheme of things was just to be creative and not to actually create something. That is why creating something need not be considered as the only hallmark of creativity. This difference is not readily visible to our mortal eyes.

In a spiritual sense, the only goal of human life is self-realization. That is the only and ultimate objective of life. If we have reached this goal, it hardly matters whether we have created any literature or not. In contrast, if we have created a lot of literature and have done good work for society, but have not had self-realization, it is not worth anything at all. It is not essential that we are known through our literature or our work.

Self-realization may or may not be followed by a tangible creation. But it certainly brings us a lot of joy, profound peace of mind, a deep sense of contentment and real meaning to our life. If we are in possession of such precious treasures, it does not matter whether we are well known or unknown in this world.

Known and Unknown Creative People

My personal experience of being in the company of so-called realized individuals who are also in the limelight has been very disappointing. They appeared less spiritually advanced to me than those who are realized but are not well known. I have noticed a definite streak of arrogance in their behaviour, because they are famous. Being prominent is a highly nourishing food for our ego, which expands as people begin to recognize us in public. Arrogance grows along with the growing ego.

In contrast, those who are not very famous or who are more or less anonymous, are extremely comfortable and completely at ease with themselves. Maybe it is because they don't have to worry about maintaining an image in the eyes of the people who gather around them. They can afford to be what they actually are. They are full of love and wisdom, which they share with those who come into contact with them. Their actions and thoughts are in total harmony with each other. Their life speaks for itself about their inner state of spiritual enlightenment. They are incredibly strong and powerful from inside, but equally polite and gentle in their demeanour. They never let others feel uncomfortable in their presence. Being warm and luminous is their very nature.

High Sensitivity Like a Poet

For proper understanding of the philosophy of yoga and to live up to the concepts described in the scriptures of yoga, what we need most is a high degree of individual sensitivity.

Poets are generally endowed with such sensitivity and therefore they are highly creative. But just because they are sensitive and creative does not mean that they have to produce poems all the time. In fact, whether they write verses or not is not so important. What is most important is to enjoy the state of creativity from where the poems really originate. The joy of creation lies more in the process than in the product.

A famous author was once interviewed on TV. During the interview he said, 'As soon as I am done with the writing of a book or a script or a verse, I prefer to get completely disconnected from the related thoughts. I do not like to waste my time thinking about how it will be received by the readers. I don't even expect them to like everything I write. Naturally, I do feel very happy when somebody tells me that he liked what I wrote. But I leave it at that and prefer to focus my attention on writing on some new subject and remain absorbed in it.'

In short, we may say that spiritual and material creativity are both quite useful and important, and we can decide which one we want most and develop it accordingly. But the best way is to develop both and strike a balance between them. Once we do that, they will help and complement each other.

SECRET NUMBER NINE

*Be Receptive to
Spiritual Grace*

Windfall Of Devotion

In recent times, it seems that people have suddenly started turning to the worship of God in a big way. All the famous temples, mosques and churches are literally flooded with devotees. The queues in front of these sacred places are growing day by day. Thousands of people go to listen to the discourses given by modern saints and self-proclaimed 'Godmen' on various topics related to God worship. TV channels also provide good coverage of different programmes on God and related topics.

By looking at the huge outburst of apparent devotion, God must be wondering whether the present times, which are supposed to be bad times, are actually bad or in fact good? He must be asking whether he inadvertently started the good cycle (*Satya Yuga*) instead of the bad one (*Kali Yuga*). 'If it was really a bad cycle as I had planned, how can there be so much of devotion? So much of outpouring of love for me? How is it possible?'

It sounds ridiculous to offer prayers to God in the hope of getting our wishes fulfilled, particularly when it is done in the form of a contract or a deal promising Him a commission or some cut if we are successful. Who is going to give a cut to whom? The whole world belongs to Him, including whatever belongs to us. So, how can we possibly give anything to Him as a gift, if it already belongs to Him?

In fact, idols like Lord Ganesh, Lord Shankar or Lord Maruti are mere symbols of the all-pervasive life principle. This principle itself is what we call God. The wise sages from the past have devised these 'symbols of infinity', because it is very difficult to comprehend the infinite vastness of this principle with our limited human minds. The symbols are useful tools for giving expression to our feelings of love and gratitude towards God. At times, when we are in deep grief, we may need external support and in such situations if we seek support from the higher power, it is somewhat justified.

Real Worship

Obviously, what is happening is nothing like real worship. It is only a very superficial expression of devotion. Real worship is establishing an intimate relationship with God and nothing more. The last thing we should do during such worship is to ask for something from Him, in return for what we have offered to Him in the form of worship.

In real worship, we are supposed to express our genuine feelings of love, respect and gratitude towards Him. We develop a natural sense of reverence and awe towards Him, when we look at the astounding degree of perfection He has achieved in all the constituent parts of His creation.

Grace is the Same for All

We need His Grace and we seek it through worship. But the Grace of God is being showered on all of us, all the time. It never falls more on one person and less on the next. It is like rain – it doesn't fall more in the fields of the rich than in the fields of the poor. It is true that a rich farmer can afford to purchase properly irrigated land, or land in an area where there is adequate rainfall. Rich farmers in India may even go one step further and pay additional money to the local authorities to get their farms irrigated in the dry seasons. The poor farmers can't afford to pay more, so their crops perish.

But God can't be held responsible for such discrimination and disparity. There isn't any difference in His Grace. We human beings are the ones that create the differences. Whether rich or poor, we all experience hunger pangs alike. There is no difference in the basic sensation of hunger in us. The difference lies only in the food we are able to eat to satisfy our appetite.

As a meditator, we have to always bear in mind that if we are receptive to the Divine Grace, it will shower on us in abundance, all the time.

Being Receptive

To be receptive to Divine Grace, we have to learn to become empty from within. It is not the emptiness which is commonly known as the 'devil's workshop'. It is a more positive, more potent, more dynamic type of emptiness. Once we are able to experience this empty state within ourselves, we don't need to do anything else to receive His Grace. In fact, as long as we are striving for His Grace, it will never come to us.

But the moment we stop worrying about getting it, the Grace begins to fall on us lavishly.

Unless we are free from the shackles of our own ego, we will not stop from being the 'doers' of everything. Unless we are liberated from the false notion of 'doer-ship', which is nurtured by our ego, we will never be truly empty. And, unless we are completely empty from the inside, we will not be able to receive the Grace properly.

There are two beautiful mythological stories from Indian literature that clearly depict the importance of being empty. One of them is about Lord Krishna. He was very dear to all. Everybody liked to be as close to Him as possible. It is said that people who loved him felt jealous of the flute which was placed directly on His lips. The flute had this special privilege because it was willing to be empty from inside. It was ready to give up its identity completely to receive the Divine breath and let it pass through it without any obstruction whatsoever.

The other story is also about Lord Krishna. Draupadi was his sister. Lord Krishna had given her a small plate as a gift. One day, she had a lot of guests at home. The food was not sufficient for them all. She was worried. But, being a true devotee of the Lord, she believed in his providence. She started serving food to the guests, with great reverence and love for them. After serving food to one guest, she emptied the plate and kept on emptying it till she served food to the next. Thus, she could feed all the guests on that day. She realized that every time she emptied the plate, it got filled up with fresh food.

These stories are not supposed to be treated as real-life stories. They are meant to highlight some interesting dimensions of our life. Both stories suggest that if our inside is filled up with thoughts, memories, deeds, emotions and all the other things related to the ego, there will be no room for anything else. If we can get beyond the clutches of our small ego, we realize that our inner world is instantly filled up with Divine Grace.

In fact, one who has too much ego needs freedom from it the most. It creates a lot of stress in such a person. When the stress becomes unbearable, they feel like being free from it. Going for a walk, chatting with a close friend, watching a television show, taking a drink and smoking are some of the ways in which they seek release. One does experience some relief from stress after indulging in one or more of these activities. Along with stress relief, one also experiences relief from the pressure caused by the ego. Such relief is only partial and temporary, but it is nevertheless a welcome relief.

This relief from the ego does create an emptiness within the person, but soon it is filled up with ego again, because usually people do not know what to do with such emptiness. The vicious cycle continues, in the form of ego, stress, partial stress relief and ego again.

In contrast, a person who has clearly understood the illusion of existence or a person who does everything as a matter of service to the Lord or a true devotee who is overfilled with love for God, is liberated from the clutches of the ego. They can therefore receive the Grace without any difficulty whatsoever. They realize God in His entirety and experience the immensity of joy of being in close proximity to Him all the time. Because of the continuous sharing of this joy with others, their heart is emptied again and again. After getting empty, it is immediately filled up with Divine Grace.

Dissolution of the Ego

Our heart can either accommodate ego or Divine Grace. If it is filled with the ego, there is no room left for Grace to come in and if it is filled with Grace, there is no space for the ego. That is why we have to make sure that we remain empty from the inside, so that the Divine Grace will continuously keep pouring into us.

A story of a holy man is very apt in this context. He was a renunciant who would go to five houses every day to ask for alms. He used to cook the food and eat it in his hermitage. It is customary in India that a renunciant who has sacrificed everything at the feet of God should be looked after well by those who are leading worldly lives. The renunciants are not supposed to own any property. They are not even supposed to stay at one place for more than three days at a stretch and should lead a very simple life. Their only mission in life is self-education and the education of others. If such a holy man comes to your doorstep and asks for food, it is considered a great opportunity and privilege to serve him well. He is never treated like a 'beggar'. He is given the best possible reception. He is respectfully invited inside the house and is served food with great reverence. A host feels very fortunate to welcome such a guest into his house.

The holy man in the story goes to a house and asks for some food. The housewife asks him to sit down and make himself comfortable. She serves some food to him and asks him for some message, some pearls of wisdom that will help her be happy in her life. He leaves the house with a promise to fulfil her wish during his next visit to her house. As promised, he calls on her after a few days and asks for alms. She asks for his pot, so that she could pour the food into it. He hands over the pot to her. She finds it dirty and filled with some waste material. She says that she cannot put anything in it because it is too dirty. After saying this, she takes the pot inside, cleans it up and brings it back with some food in it.

After a while, she reminds the holy man of his promise about giving her some guidance. He says, 'My dear child! I have already given you a very important message. It seems that you have missed it. My teaching was incorporated in what you did just now. You have noticed that when "my pot" was filled with "dirt", it could not accommodate any "food" in it. But when you "cleaned and emptied" it, the same pot could hold a lot of food in it. The food you have so lovingly offered to me.'

The holy man continued further, 'Something similar can happen with you. If you are filled with the ego-induced dirt that is produced and stored inside you, you will not be able to receive His Grace. Once your ego-induced self-centred activities come to an end, your mind will become clean and empty. Then you will be able to receive the blessings of God without any difficulty.'

Appendices

Techniques of Meditation

Once we have made up our mind to learn and practise meditation, we will find that there are numerous techniques to choose from. Over a period of time, we may evolve our own methods of meditation, which are different from those of others. However, the essential nature and underlying principles of all techniques remain the same.

In this section, we will go into the three important techniques of meditation that I love the most. They are very easy to understand and simple to practise. They are (i) Shavasan-Meditation, (ii) Finding the real answer to the question 'Who am I?' and (iii) Experiencing the Inner Stillness.

1

Shavasan-Meditation (S.M.)

This is the most novel and easy technique of meditation. It was first conceived and evolved by me during my one-month stay in the sacred Himalayas for deep and intense meditation in 1973, immediately after my medical internship. This technique is blessed by the highly evolved spiritual masters from the holy mountains. I have taught it to thousands of my students from India and abroad ever since.

A book about this technique was first published in 1978 in the Marathi Indian language. It was prefaced by the then Prime Minister of India, the late Hon. Mr Morarjibhai Desai. Now it is in its twelfth edition.

While practising Shavasan-Meditation, one has to lie comfortably on the floor and go through certain stages to reach the final state of no-thought awareness.

We may get easily discouraged from learning and practising conventional forms of meditation because we have to face numerous problems right from the start. One of the most important is our inability to sit in one pose – whether simple or difficult like the lotus pose – with a straight back.

Most people from the West are not even able to sit on the ground for a few minutes, let alone for a longer period of time in meditation. If we experience such a problem at the very first step of learning meditation, we may quickly lose interest. Subsequent lack of motivation will make meditation a boring affair. Naturally, we will not be able to pursue it for a long time. As the effects of meditation become evident only after several months of sincere practice, we may deprive ourselves of the immense joy we could have experienced through meditation.

As sitting on the floor is difficult, beginners have to strain themselves during meditation. This discomfort does not permit them to transcend body awareness. This can be compared with the level of discomfort experienced while travelling in a crowded train, where we can hardly relax. It is often said that the practice of meditation requires perseverance, grit and determination, but these virtues are surely not meant for sitting in an uneasy posture, fighting pains in different parts of the body. Many teachers attach undue importance to sitting posture and literally force their students through the grind of meditation. As expected, the poor students end up with higher stress levels than before.

In Shavasan-Meditation (S.M.) we are supposed to lie on the floor in a very comfortable position. It allows us to be in that posture for a long period of time without any discomfort or pain. Thus we can easily transcend body awareness, followed by mind awareness and subsequently experience a thought-free state. That is why we can learn and practise S.M. very easily, regardless of whether we are 14 or 80 years old.

There is one more valid reason for practising meditation in a comfortable position of the body: meditation is an inner state of no-thought awareness, and it hardly matters whether our body is in a sitting position or is comfortably lying on the floor. One more advantage of S.M. is the minimum amount of time required for the mind to become completely silent. In today's busy world, every minute saved matters.

Unfortunately, many people honestly believe that they are supposed to endure pain and discomfort without a whimper of protest during meditation. The reality is very different and more beautiful.

The essence of meditation is to develop a cordial and comfortable relationship with ourselves. As mentioned elsewhere in this book, the first step is very important, because it decides the direction of the following steps. Being comfortable right from the beginning makes sense in this context too. In S.M., our body is lying comfortably on the ground – we are not forcing it to do anything, but are actually trying to be very friendly and co-operative with it. It starts responding equally well. With this approach, we begin to enjoy meditation and over a period of time we naturally start developing a taste for it. Once we start liking our meditation, further progress on the path becomes very easy.

Success Inspires, Encourages

S.M. gives an early experience and a taste of success in meditation. This early success becomes a source of encouragement and inspiration for the long term. Modern psychologists say that if young children get an early taste of success, their interest in studies automatically grows. It is therefore necessary that a child is encouraged to think that if they study well, they are capable of doing well in any subject.

Psychologists recommend that if children are initially taught the fundamental but very simple and easy to understand concepts of a subject, soon they develop a feeling that they can understand the subject well. Naturally, they will feel confident in themselves. Once they develop confidence, things become much easier for their teachers: they can play a facilitator's role and provide guidance whenever needed by the child. With self-confidence, a true liking for the subject, early experience of success and timely guidance from a supportive teacher, a child can learn more complex concepts in a given subject with far less difficulty.

First Step Should Be Easy

This is all applicable in meditation too. It is very important that we start getting positive results as early as possible. Being able to say 'I can meditate' is of paramount importance, as far as our progress in the field is concerned.

The most important thing is to reach a state of no-thought awareness through meditation. As no-thought awareness grows, the inner joy also grows proportionately. Initially, we are likely to fall asleep while doing S.M., but after some practice, this tendency automatically reduces.

With the help of S.M. we can experience freedom from thoughts, expanding awareness, bliss and effort-free naturalness. Many people have learned this technique from my associates, my colleagues and me, and have benefited immensely from regular practice. I am sure the reader will also benefit in the same manner. Best of luck!

Stage One
Wear loose-fitting comfortable clothes. Lie comfortably on the floor in a supine position (on your back). Keep your legs spread, about one and a half feet apart, with the feet turned outwards. Keep your arms away from the side of your body, with your hands about one foot away from your sides. Keep your head in a comfortable position either in the centre or turned to either the left or right side.

Stage Two
Internalize your attention and locate tensions in different parts of the body, starting with your feet and ascending right up to your head. Give enough time to each part of the body, to be aware of the tensions there. Once you notice tensions, release them by gently moving that part a little bit, until your whole body is completely relaxed and tension-free.

Stage Three
After lying comfortably in the position described above, gently turn your attention to your chest and observe how it automatically rises and falls with each normal act of breathing. Don't control or concentrate on your breath. Just be aware of the movement of your chest.

Stage Four
Turn your attention to all the thoughts that keep coming to your mind all the time. Just let them come, stay and go according to their natural tendency. You should neither fight against certain thoughts nor get carried away with others. Keep witnessing all these thoughts without having any personal reaction to them.

Some Tips:

- Do this in the morning, preferably before your breakfast, for about 10–15 minutes.
- Repeat it twice in the evening – firstly after you return from work, and secondly when you are in bed ready to sleep.
- If possible, do it before lunch in the office too. Maybe just for five minutes, sitting in a chair in a semi-reclined position or stretching your body with your head resting against the wall.
- Don't be in a hurry to enter the state of meditation or rush to come out of it. Do everything at a leisurely pace.
- Don't worry if you fall asleep in the beginning. Later on the quality of your regular sleep during night will improve and the hours of sleep will decrease.

2

'Who Am I?'

This technique involves asking a very simple question, 'Who am I?', and exploring it thoroughly to find the real answer about who we actually are. It is rather a strange kind of question one could ask and start looking for the answer within oneself.

The question must be asked and answered with utmost sincerity, honesty and intensity. Bhagwan Ramana Maharshi, the great sage of India, made this form of meditation popular. It is a very simple type of meditation that is easy to understand and practice, irrespective of any religion. Finding a true answer to this question is really a great challenge.

'Am I What I Look Like?'

It requires a great deal of perseverance and patience to find a real answer to the question, 'Who am I?' We need tremendous motivation to pursue this question to the end.

Everybody knows how intelligent, how handsome or how capable one is. At least, it is possible to know about these things without too much difficulty. But very few of us know what we actually are. There is a difference between our knowledge of what we are and the understanding of others about how we look to them. Our worldly affairs are governed and controlled more by our notion about ourselves than what we actually are. In general, we are not aware of our real self because we are never introduced to it.

If we do not discover our unmanifest and not easily perceptible real 'I', our life remains based on a weak foundation. All our thoughts, emotions, actions and behaviour are structured on this weak foundation, and we will naturally tend to remain unstable

175

and insecure. The inner sense of instability and insecurity keeps continuously affecting our worldly life.

Knowing Oneself is Very Important

To develop an urge to know our 'true' self, we have to become thoroughly dissatisfied with all that we are doing with the help of our 'false' self. Unfortunately, most people do not have enough courage to be completely dissatisfied like this. Unless we are able to actually experience the extreme suffering of such dissatisfaction, we will never develop enough motivation to explore what real happiness is.

That is why most people waste their valuable life in getting tossed between 'lukewarm happiness' on one hand and 'lukewarm suffering' on the other. Ultimately, as we reach the end of our life, we suddenly realize that we have achieved many things, like going through higher education, earning lots of money and recognition, but within us we are still not truly happy, satisfied and contented. This is the tragedy of many older people: they experience a sense of frustration and emptiness for having wasted their life chasing after and accumulating unimportant things, then due to old age they no longer have enough energy to lead their life differently.

It is therefore necessary that we start working towards our real goal while we are still very young. We should develop an intense urge to ask the fundamental question, 'Who am I?' and start pursuing it in earnest from our youth. We have to remember that even if the whole world seems to know us well but if we don't know our true self well, it is worth nothing at all. On the other hand, if we know our true self well, but the world doesn't know us at all, this is of greater value and significance.

Ignorance – Root Cause of All Problems

Whenever we face grave problems and do not find proper solutions to them, we may suddenly realize that the real cause of all our problems and our suffering is that we do not know ourselves well enough. Once we know that self-ignorance is the main cause of our problems, we develop a genuine need to remove our ignorance and start doing something concrete, by asking, 'Who am I?' with all our heart and mind involved in the question.

It is Not a Mere Verbal Question

If there isn't enough intensity and earnestness in asking this question, it is reduced to a superficial verbal question. If the question is superficial, the answer is bound to be trivial. Verbal solutions are not the real answers to this question. The urge to get the real answer to this question should become the top priority in our life. Interestingly, we will not get the real answer to this question unless it is asked properly.

In worldly life many things depend on how we ask a particular question. If a young man who is in love with a girl proposes to her in a dry tone, she is bound to turn down his proposal. For a girl, the asking of the question is not so important. She is far more concerned about the manner in which it is asked and with what level of sincerity it is asked. Her answer depends on these things more than anything else. In fact, if a young man is truly in love, he will not need to put it into words to convey his feelings. His sweetheart will realize his genuine love, without his telling her about it.

Compared with other trivial questions of life, 'Who am I?' happens to be a very special kind of question. It occupies our whole life and becomes the most valuable question we could possibly ask ourselves. If it is not, it should be.

Nothing is going to be achieved if it is asked mechanically. Moreover, nothing is going to happen if we spend our entire life repeating this question hundreds of thousands of times. Chanting it mechanistically will be a total waste of time and energy. However, if it is asked just once with great intensity and integrity, that will be enough. It will stay with us in the deeper layers of our being forever and it will keep influencing our life from there on, in a very subtle manner.

'Are We Our Relations?'

Many people are under the wrong impression that they don't need to ask this question at all, because they think they already know the answer.

'What is so difficult about knowing myself?' is their usual response. They believe that they are the son of their parents, husband of their wife, father of their children, manager in a company, and so on and so on. The problem is how can a single person handle all these relations? There should be several 'I's to take care of them all.

Our experience suggests that although these relations belong to the 'I', the relations are not the real 'I'. The real 'I' is certainly different from the relationships – it is present in the relations, but it is not only to be found there; it exists apart from these relations too. It is similar to what we do with our sense organs. We make use of our eyes to see, ears to hear, tongue to taste, nose to smell and skin to touch, but these sense organs by themselves are not our true 'I'.

Even when performing all these functions, our 'I' remains separate from all these sensations. If it were not so, we would be divided into many 'I's, instead of one 'I'. But it doesn't happen that way.

When we are fast asleep, we are not aware that 'I' is a particular person, with a particular name and form. But when we wake up, we immediately know that we exist. Not only that, we also know if we have slept well. How can we say that we were not present during sleep? This means that our 'I' was present during sleep too. We may say that the real purpose behind asking the question 'Who am I?', is to understand that our 'I' during wakeful hours is the same as our 'I' during sound sleep.

The Search for 'I' Should be Without Any Prejudices

It is very important that we observe certain precautions while asking the question. First of all, we have to wholeheartedly concede that we don't really know what our real 'I' is and that is the reason why we want to do the search.

Naturally, if we don't know our 'I', we should not waste our time thinking about it or forming preconceived notions about how our real self 'should' be or will be. It would be foolish to do so, because however great the imaginary notion about our 'I' may be, it can never replace our real 'I'. Why do it then?

As a part of spiritual practice, some spiritual masters recommend that we should constantly remind ourselves by saying 'I am the blissful spirit' or 'I am a bright light'. But by merely repeating these words, we will never be able to experience the luminosity or blissfulness of the spirit. In fact, it may actually prove to be a big obstacle if we do that.

The best thing to do is to ask the question with utmost sincerity without getting lost in any form of imagination whatsoever and just leave it at that. We will usually have to wait a long time before we reach the real answer – the answer to this question is as special as the question is. When we get the answer, we will realize that it is truly a very unusual answer.

Waiting for the Real Answer

Once we have asked this question properly, it will enter into the deepest parts of our being. It will completely take charge of our mind, body, intellect and emotions. The greater the intensity of the question, the nearer will be the answer. Paradoxically, if we are prepared to wait, the answer will come faster than expected, but if we are impatient it will take much longer.

It is similar to a seed that is sown in the ground. If we want the seed to germinate, we have to sow it and wait for some time until it starts sprouting. Just as the seed doesn't germinate immediately after it is sown, the seed of this question also doesn't germinate instantly after it is sown in the field of our mind.

We have to trust that, under favourable conditions, the seed that is sown in the soil will germinate in few days. If we worry too much about its sprouting, or keep digging every day to confirm its germination, we will surely destroy the seed. Similarly, once we sow the seed of the question 'Who am I?' inside us, we have to water it with prejudice-free searching, remove all the weeds of imagination on time, offer it the fertilizer of intense urge and provide enough air and water of patience for it to sprout early.

Whenever we get the real answer, we will not be able to recognize it as we do with our usual questions and their usual answers. In fact, if we recognize the answer to this question, the chances are that it is not the real answer.

This is probably the only question in the whole world to which when we get the real answer we don't know it in the conventional sense of the term. Still, we certainly get the answer and also feel very confident that we have got it. With long-term effort and patience, the answer automatically comes to us in an uninvited manner.

After having got the real answer, our life fills to the brim with immense joy. Life becomes far more meaningful than before. We become free of all kinds of stress. We begin to enjoy absolute peace of mind and immeasurable happiness.

3

An Experience of Absolute Stillness

This technique of meditation is based on the teachings of the great philosopher and world teacher, J. Krishnamurti. It is a very subtle method of meditation that explains the importance of having a raw experience of every sensation, without using any words to describe it.

For example, if we eat an apple and we want to explain its taste to one of our friends, we will say, 'The apple was very tasty.' Similarly, while describing a beautiful scene, we have to make use of words. Imagine a situation in which we had the experience of the sweet taste of the apple and of the beauty of nature, but there was nobody around us with whom we could talk about our experiences. In a situation like that, it would be quite absurd on our part to start describing them to ourselves. We already know through our experience what we are going to talk about. There is absolutely no need to use any words to describe the experiences to ourselves. If we make use of words, it will only affect the purity of our initial experiences.

Pure Experience Beyond Words

The sweet taste of an apple is its nature, whether we use any words to describe its sweetness to anybody else or not. Its taste remains the same whether we call it sweet or bitter or sour, or don't say anything. The apple will taste the same to a person who is able to use words to describe its taste and a person who is dumb. The experience of the sweet taste is the same for both. Similarly, the experience of the beauty of nature will be the same for them both, but one will not be able to share his experience with others and the other may paint a beautiful picture, or write an article or a poem about the experience.

To have a raw experience we don't need any words. Words are necessary only when we share our experience with others. I know that I have to make use of words to say that words are not necessary to have a raw experience of something.

Knowing this, we have to make sure that we don't let any words interfere with any of our direct experiences. We have to use words with caution. Use them only when it is absolutely necessary, but avoid their use whenever they are not needed.

Unfortunately, most of us cannot differentiate between pure experience and its verbal description. That is why we tend to use words while having a pure experience of something, and by doing so we actually spoil the purity of the experience.

Experiential Knowledge

We have to always keep it in mind that the knowledge we are going to gain after regular practice of meditation is purely subjective experiential knowledge and not the conventional type of material knowledge. Many great sages and seers have endeavoured to describe their higher experiences to us. But none of them have so far been able to describe them fully and nobody will ever be able to do it in the future, because those experiences are essentially subjective in nature and are beyond all descriptions.

As we can experience the sweet taste of an apple without using any words to describe it, we can do this with other experiences too. Over a period of time, we become conversant with the process of having a silent experience of everything. Slowly, making use of the same process, we can get an experiential knowledge of our true self.

Words are necessary for knowledge of the external world, but they are not at all necessary for inner experiences. We don't need to have command over any language to know our true self. But we certainly need it to do well in the external world.

While practising this technique of meditation, we can make use of all our sense organs. Krishnamurti used to talk about 'just seeing' and 'just listening'. If we learn how to take every experience the way it comes to us, without contaminating its purity with any thoughts or words, in due course we develop great insight into ourselves. Such insight is in fact, the true self-knowledge.

Raw Experience of Delivering a Child

A few years ago, a pregnant patient came to our Yoga Clinic to learn yoga for pain-free delivery. I told her that as this was her first experience of delivering a baby, she should keep her mind open to face the situation as it comes and not carry any preconceived notions about it. I suggested that she go through this unique experience boldly, freely and with an open mind. If the delivery is going to be painful, I said, it will be so. Why worry about it? If it is painful, let it be so. Go through the pure experience of pain as and when it comes. Do not carry any thoughts about it. At the time when you go into labour, just experience whatever happens in full awareness. Don't analyse or resist the experience when it comes.

As expected, she had a normal delivery. She had some pain during the delivery, but it was bearable.

In fact, the pain of childbirth largely depends on the woman's mental state. If, during pregnancy, she is constantly exposed to negative thoughts about painful delivery, she approaches childbirth with a fearful mind and therefore suffers much pain. If she receives proper mental training and knows what to expect and how to face the situation, it helps minimize pain to a large extent. Now, we get many pregnant women coming to our Yoga Clinic to learn about pain-free delivery through yoga.

Experience of Pure and Raw Sensations

We can try one more experiment. Whenever we experience some sensation in the body, we have to just stay with that sensation, without trying to explain it in words. If we are hungry, just experience the pure sensation of hunger, without using the word 'hunger'. Do not think about eating anything to satisfy the hunger sensation. Just stay with the pure sensation of hunger.

I suggested this experiment to one of my obese patients. To my surprise, he came back after a few months and I could not recognize him. He reported that a few days after he started having the raw experience of hunger sensation, he realized that there was a vast difference between a 'false' hunger sensation and the 'real' one. He also realized that he had put on weight not because of over-eating, but because of his inability to differentiate between true and false hunger. It also occurred to him that what he was responding to was not the real sensation of hunger, but to thoughts and words about the sensation. Naturally, he used to eat more than he needed. Now he eats only when he is truly hungry and not when he gets a false hunger sensation. Later, his false hunger was substantially reduced and his sense and understanding of true hunger improved. He could keep his food intake and weight under control without any difficulty whatsoever, without the need to go on any crash diets.

Once we are capable of going through all our experiences in this manner, our experiential understanding about ourselves grows. With this understanding at our disposal, we can make excellent progress in meditation.

WATKINS

Sharing Wisdom Since
1893

The story of Watkins Publishing dates back to March 1893, when John M. Watkins, a scholar of esotericism, overheard his friend and teacher Madame Blavatsky lamenting the fact that there was nowhere in London to buy books on mysticism, occultism or metaphysics. At that moment Watkins was born, soon to become the home of many of the leading lights of spiritual literature, including Carl Jung, Rudolf Steiner, Alice Bailey and Chögyam Trungpa.

Today our passion for vigorous questioning is still resolute. With over 350 titles on our list, Watkins Publishing reflects the development of spiritual thinking and new science over the past 120 years. We remain at the cutting edge, committed to publishing books that change lives.

DISCOVER MORE ...

Read our blog

Watch and listen to
our authors in action

Sign up to
our mailing list

JOIN IN THE CONVERSATION

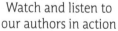

Our books celebrate conscious, passionate, wise and happy living.
Be part of the community by visiting

www.watkinspublishing.com